1

John D. Rockefeller

The Original Titan

John D. Rockefeller

The Original Titan

Insight and Analysis into the Life of the
Richest Man in American History

JR MacGregor

John D. Rockefeller – The Original Titan

Copyright © 2019 JR MacGregor

Published by CAC Publishing LLC

ISBN 978-1-950010-31-8 paperback

ISBN 978-1-950010-30-1 eBook

Contents

Introduction...7
Chapter 1 Early Years..21
Chapter 2 The Civil War...57
Chapter 3 Titusville...64
Chapter 4 Rockefeller Meets Oil 73
Chapter 5 Strategic Mindset...................................104
Chapter 6 Family..110
Chapter 7 Standard Oil...115
Chapter 8 Monopolies, Electricity, and Alcohol ...121
Chapter 9 Heir to the Throne 127
Chapter 10 The Three Titans 133
Chapter 11 Ida Tarbell 138
Chapter 12 Pipelines, Railroads, and Corruption...145
Chapter 13 Philanthropy 153
Chapter 14 The Final Chapter in Greatness...........165
Conclusion 169

Introduction

> "If your only goal is to become rich, you will never achieve it."
>
> **— John D. Rockefeller**

John D. Rockefeller made two wishes when he was young: to make $100,000 and to live one hundred years. He accomplished neither. He made significantly more that he could have imagined, and he only lived until he was ninety-seven.

John D. Rockefeller, oil titan and founder of the Standard Oil Company, was a man of great intelligence, character, and perseverance. He came from an extremely uncomfortable and shameful background yet succeeded in becoming one of the world's richest men in modern times. At the highest point in his life, prior to his full-fledged philanthropy, John D. Rockefeller was worth almost $650 billion in inflation-adjusted dollars. That is almost five times more than the richest person alive today and 1.5 percent of the entire U.S. economy.

Rockefeller's start was not one of inheritance or comfort. His father, a quack doctor who was also a con man, never gave John money that he didn't ask to be returned or loaned him money without interest. Rockefeller never received any inheritance from him. Every single penny that Rockefeller amassed throughout his he earned himself.

Rockefeller's father treated him like the outside world treated a stranger. Rockefeller learned from him the strategies of business but disliked him so much that when his mother passed he asked the minister who took care of the funeral to describe her as a widow. Despite his rough background, not only did he go on to become one of the most successful people in the world and the richest man in modern times, but he also went on to fuel the building of America with his oil.

Rockefeller's humble beginnings, religious background, dysfunctional father, and pious mother molded him into a man who took business very seriously, saved every penny, and was morally upright.

He was accused of being unscrupulous for how he built up Standard Oil. Some accused him from a position of truth, while others accused him because they were jealous that he was rich. After all, no one likes the rich guy. Everyone is jealous of a wealthy person and will say and do anything to criticize them. It's true that he may have done some seemingly unethical things now and then, but how do you define ethical in the grand scheme of things? After all, you can't make an omelet without breaking a few eggs.

To really understand the depth of his success, you need to put it into context and imagine what the country and the rest of the world for that matter was like just after the Civil War. You also have to take into consideration that transportation infrastructure was not as effective as it is today and that the industries we take for granted, including education, banking, and shipping, were nowhere near what they are today.

You should also consider the influences in his life. Rockefeller was a pious Baptist who adhered to the moral principles of not drinking and not indulging in pleasures of the flesh. He was deeply affected by the excesses of his father and chose to, viscerally, lead a life of piety, purity, and honor. For those who think that his life of wealth and cutthroat competition invalidate his religious views, you will see in this book that that is not the way Rockefeller saw it.

He never had a problem working with others, and he is often quoted as saying that he would rather reap the benefits of collaboration than put in all the work himself. He was certainly a master of hard work, but he was the king of delegating. He knew that each person had his own area of expertise and that more hands were better than one. It is also one of the reasons why his expansion of oil refineries was not just built one at a time but pooled together by acquisition. In this and other ways, he was a genius in terms of seeing the outcome of various strategies of collaboration.

His life was connected with those of the other titans of America, from steel magnate Andrew Carnegie to financial titan and king of finance, J.P. Morgan. He was highly competitive and didn't stop at just one way of advancing his company. If he saw potential in making money from his fellow titans, he was not one to hesitate in taking advantage of it. To some, like the milder-mannered Carnegie, this was uncouth and unacceptable. Rockefeller never hesitated to jump on an idea, and neither was he hesitant to work hard to see it come to fruition. He was never afraid of putting in the effort and trying, but once he started, he didn't allow failure to daunt him or torture him into giving up. He worked hard to create the empire that he built from nothing, and he was a hardworking, persevering, and fearless man who conquered the world.

John D. Rockefeller was a man of solid moral character in the midst of a country that was playing it fast and loose. America in the 1800s had its wild streak, but Rockefeller was not a participant. His views on temperance and partying were absolute, and he was not distracted.

He used intelligence, drive, and perseverance to manifest his goals. As a youth, he worked tenaciously when employed as a bookkeeper and went on to trade produce during the Civil War. It would be rather odd to say that he profited greatly from the Civil War, but that is the truth. He supported Lincoln, but the politics of Lincoln's cause was not reason enough for him to avoid profiting from it. J.P Morgan had profited from it just as Andrew Carnegie did as well.

His fortune was certainly built from the sweat of his brow and the spark of his mind. Although people accused him of unscrupulous ways as they did with fellow titan, J.P. Morgan, they never really understood the process of his mind and the benefit of his actions. You have to look beyond the cloud of his wealth to appreciate the benefit of his actions. Without Rockefeller, the oil industry would not have become what it is today and would not have been there to fuel the expansion and prominence of the United States on the world's stage. Significant geopolitical forces arose directly from the consolidation of the refineries and the way Rockefeller conducted his business.

His prowess as a businessman was well known, and that was not just in the United States. Across the world, such people as Ludvig Nobel feared the might and power of Rockefeller as he attempted to expand his oil business originating from the Caspian Sea. Rockefeller, after conquering the oil industry in the United States, had made a name for himself internationally, and his reputation was certainly questionnable.

If you are a student of history, you can't help but see that such men as Rockefeller and Morgan worked very hard for the wealth and power they amassed. It wasn't easy. Because of the power and wealth they accumulated, people did not appreciate their contribution but enjoyed living in the world that was built by them. Rockefeller has been dead for almost a century (he died in 1937), yet we still live in a world shaped by the economics of his endeavors in oil.

It was not by accident or fate that we use petroleum in cars today instead of electricity and ethanol. Both were available as a source of fuel when automobiles became the mainstream mode of transportation. It was by the will of Rockefeller.

Rockefeller's business strategies and tactics were simple: do whatever was needed to get what he wanted (and never use money as the goal). Any smart entrepreneur, businessman, or upstart should remember that if they want to become successful. Henry Ford had the same principles. In fact, if he had wanted to make more money, he may have decided to make expensive cars. If that was the path he chose, he would not have become the Henry Ford we know today. He wasn't looking to make money. He was looking to make cars for the masses. Rockefeller wasn't looking to make money; if he did, he wouldn't have reinvested his profits to buy up more refineries.

Despite Rockefeller's vast wealth, he was very thrifty. He raised his children to not be indulgent, and he wasn't either. He spent his money only when he saw that the outcome would be the best. If the outcome was not beneficial, he would not spend a single cent. In fact, he would go around the house at night extinguishing the lamps around the house so that he would be able to save on kerosene. He didn't want to waste, and that desire to not waste resulted in his desire for efficiency. After all, what is efficiency if not the desire to not waste?

Rockefeller was a man of few words but a master negotiator. Negotiation has two elements: using the power of words (the precise and articulate use of them) and being able to twist someone's arm without breaking it. Rockefeller had copious amounts of both.

He built his business through negotiation, hard work, coercion, and, yes, even "corruption," creating an oil behemoth so large that if you add up all the companies that were once part of the original Standard Oil it would eclipse even the largest company in existence today. Rockefeller's Standard Oil Company was not just about oil refining. It was a symbol of power, strength, and cunning.

Even though Rockefeller created a vast business empire and altered the standing of the United States in the world, his unpopularity was often why politicians attacked him in the name of the people. People did not like his methods or his strategies. In 1911, the U.S. government called for the breakup of Standard Oil because they accused him of having built a monopoly. Instead of being defeated, he took the companies that were broken by the government and built several giant corporations from the fragments of Standard Oil. That led to the creation of some of the largest oil companies in the world today—Exxon and Mobil—to name just two.

The man behind Standard Oil was someone who changed the way the world worked. He propelled the oil industry from a nascent posture to what it is today. It would not be this way if it weren't for him.

John D. Rockefeller was a cold and expressionless man in his early years. When surrounded by his family, he displayed a fun-loving nature. He was happiest when he was out cycling with his children. In his sunset years, he was a genial old man who gave dimes to people. He loved children and raised them to be religious, morally upright, and not interested in pleasures of the flesh.

Rockefeller was a very personal man, preferring not to talk about his business. Perhaps he just didn't like talking about things of the sort. He attended to business when he had to and during other times did not really tend to it much.

Finally, John D. Rockefeller was a man who revolutionized thought. Business schools across the country still teach budding industrialists and managers the way to think about business—something that came naturally to Rockefeller. He was an example for people to follow who want to make a fortune for themselves in business. Truly successful people like John D. Rockefeller do not care for niceties or regulations—only about accomplishing what they set their sights on.

Before Rockefeller entered the oil industry, the American people were relying on whale oil, lard oil, and other fuels for illuminants. They used coal as a source of energy and power. During his early years, crude oil was discovered. It was a black sludge seen as gold, and enterprising businessmen thought it would lead to immense fortune.

At the beginning of the oil industry, the better part of the United States lacked proper illuminants. Whale oil was becoming increasingly expensive since it was harder to find and harvest. The poor and middle-income people could not really afford these expensive illuminants, leaving only the rich with the luxury of having light when it was dark.

The first popular product that sprung from the oil industry was a new illuminant. The black, or sometimes yellow, crude oil, depending on where it's found, could be distilled, refined, or as it was known back then, cleansed, to become kerosene, the perfect illuminant. Kerosene was cheap and easily affordable for the masses. It was both suitable for the people and profitable for sellers and producers.

John D. Rockefeller entered the oil industry with a plan to fortify it and control it himself. Before Rockefeller, in the infant days of the industry, people feared that the oil supply would run out, and panic ensued when wells went dry. Unlike most people, however, Rockefeller saw that the oil industry was not going to fizzle away. He knew it would last, and he acted upon his beliefs, creating the first trillion-dollar corporation, Standard Oil Trust.

Rockefeller transformed America, being the largest producer of kerosene and oil-related products in the United States.

Over the last two centuries or so, the coal industry has been dwindling, and it would be impractical to revert to it. Now, the two dominant power sources in the world are gasoline, or oil, and electricity.

Rockefeller changed the U.S. economy, making the country one whose industries and businesses used oil. When the automobile industry boomed, the market for gasoline, which, in turn, means the market for crude oil, soared.

All of that was probably only possible because of John D. Rockefeller.

Chapter 1 Early Years

"If you want to succeed you should strike out on new paths, rather than travel the worn paths of accepted success."

— John D. Rockefeller

John Davison Rockefeller's grandfather was Godfrey Rockefeller, who married an English lady, the descendent of a European king. Her name was Lucy. She was very strong. Rockefeller later said she was stronger than his grandfather. By marrying Godfrey, Lucy was actually marrying a family of lower class. At the time, the Rockefellers were just a bunch of drunken rogues worth nothing.

Godfrey and Lucy had ten children, the third of which was William Avery Rockefeller, the father of John D. Rockefeller. From a very young age, William was a solitary person, sometimes wandering off on his own and not returning home for long stretches of time.

The Rockefeller family eventually settled in Richford, New York, while they were on their way to Michigan. There was an obstacle in their path, a hill to be exact, and they could not go any farther. So, they settled down for a life in Richford.

William grew up to be a con man, scheming and swindling people to make money. He was also a lecherous man who committed several appalling acts in his life.

To pull off his schemes, he would ride into a new town with a sign hanging from his buttonhole that informed people that he was deaf and dumb. This allowed him to get close to strangers and listen to their conversations to learn many of their secrets. He would then use those secrets to manipulate them or find ways to sell things to those people and profit.

He was also obnoxious and arrogant in his deception. One family that William had appraoched to sell things accepted him into their home, and he and the family became close. One day the mistress of the house saw William talking to someone in the market. When she confronted him, he easily lied and told her that he had miraculously been healed that morning.

Eventually, William fell in love with one Miss Nancy Brown. The two of them planned to marry. They dated for some time, and all the plans were made, but an intervening event altered the course of those plans.

William had heard about another lady, a Ms. Eliza Davison, who was an heiress to a wealthy family. Rumor had it that her father was to give her $500 as a wedding gift. William decided that marrying Ms. Davison would be a better deal than marrying Ms. Brown.

William proposed to Eliza, who was overwhelmed with excitement but said she would marry William only if he was not deaf and dumb. He then miraculously regained use of his voice and hearing.

Eliza's father strictly disapproved of their marriage, but she disobeyed him and the two of them wed. After the wedding, William took her to his home in Richford, a simple, rectangular shack with one awning at the side.

Not wanting to leave the love of his life twisting in the wind, he decided to employ her as their housekeeper. William eventually fathered children with both of them. In two years, he had four children, one of which was John D. Rockefeller, born July 8, 1839, in Richford, New York, to the first Mrs. Rockefeller.

The illegitimate children of William and Nancy were both daughters, one of whom died young, and the other grew up to become a schoolteacher. The one who survived never met John, and it is probable that John did not know of the existence of his two half-sisters at all.

When Rockefeller was very young, the Rockefeller family (and Nancy) moved to Moravia for some time and then later to Owego, where he studied at the Owego Academy. William often deserted his family, leaving for months at a time, and Eliza would be forced to take care of the household without any income.

He also did the same to the family he had with Nancy.

In frustration, Nancy began to argue with both Eliza and William. Unsure of how much longer he could keep the cat in the bag, he sent Nancy and their two daughters away to live at a friend's house. He didn't completely abandon them and would sometimes place clothing at their front door. The rest was up to Nancy.

Rockefeller did not remember much about his life in Richford before they moved to Moravia. Rockefeller was close to his father at first, but he despised him as he grew older and came to understand what his father was really like. He would later fear having to rely on him, which pushed him to seek his own independence.

Eliza was also not very happy with her marriage. She now understood that she had made the wrong choice by marrying her husband and not heeding her father's advice. She became suspicious about what William was doing while he was away and was miserable. She remained silent, though, keeping what she thought he might be doing in her heart so as to spare her children the pain and suffering of a dishonest father.

Eliza tended to the farm, and the children were given their own chores to do. Later, however, William would get someone to tend to the farm for Eliza and her children. John and his siblings slept in a room heated only by a small pipe in one section of the room. In the morning, the sounds of the town coming alive with people bustling about would waken the tired children and get them to their feet, and the entire family had their share of work to do.

John's morning chore, among other things, was to milk the cow. For warmth, he would stand on the same spot the cow stood to warm his feet.

After much harassment by his wife about leaving the family unattended for months at a time, William told the local shopkeeper to let Eliza and the family take anything they wanted, and he would settle the debt when he returned from his business trips.

This at least gave Eliza a source of food and groceries for the children, but when the amount owed began to pile up, Eliza, fearing that the credit might come to an end, became very frugal. It was a constant fear that she later pounded into her children, telling them, "Willful waste makes woeful want."

Eliza was very strong in character and personality, like her mother-in-law, Lucy. In the beginning, Eliza had been very uncomfortable around her husband's relatives, and Lucy, being the most respected of them all, became Eliza's sanctuary, and she would often be with her.

Many of the Rockefeller family's relatives admired Eliza, saying that she was an extraordinarily strong woman who was able to put up with the difficulties of her life. Despite her strange marriage, she never deserted her family and never left her husband even when the opportunity presented itself. The Rockefeller family was so poor that their neighbor had to drive them to church and buy textbooks for the children.

When John was young, he already began to show signs of enterprise. By buying small amounts of candy, portioning them, and then selling them to his siblings, he was able to make a profit. Another childhood business venture of his was to steal a turkey if it wandered away from its owner. He would catch it, take it back, and raise it for his family. His mother furnished him with milk curds, which he could use to feed the turkeys.

Rockefeller's mother was sharp and alert. Once when she was suffering from whooping cough, a disease common in those days, she kept herself in her room so as to not pass it to her children. She heard burglars one night, and knowing there was no one to protect her children, she cautiously opened her bedroom window and sang a popular Negro tune, making it appear that others were in the house and everyone was still up. The burglars heard the singing and left empty-handed.

Whenever William returned from his wandering, he would spend lavishly and give his family a good time. John would be happy to be with his father and came to associate money with good times.

Eliza eventually hired Anne Vanderbeak to help take care of the house. Unfortunately, William sexually assaulted Anne, and the family was forced to run from the law, which is when they moved to Owego.

This incident ruined the already shaky relationship between William and his father-in-law, John Davison. When William asked John for money to help with his troubles, Davison declined, which caused William to fly off the handle, and he threatened to leave and never return. John then worried about earlier loans he had made to William that were still outstanding. Fearing that he would not see that money again, John sued his son-in-law for $1,210.75. John then went on to edit his will, stipulating that Eliza would not have full control of her inheritance, and that upon her death the money would not pass to William.

It was after this incident that young John D. Rockefeller would come to despise his father, and psychoanalysts have said that he grew emotionless and calm. It had even reached the point the John had urges to kill his own father because of the humiliation and utter madness his father seemed to display.

After the issue with Miss Vanderbeak, William left the Rockefeller family in Cleveland. He needed to escape the law and get as far away as possible from those who knew him. His crime was known throughout the valley. He left John, his siblings, and his mother to fend for themselves in an unfamiliar environment. The children and their mother settled in Cleveland, which is where Rockefeller attended high school and later met his future wife, Laura Celestia Spelman, also known as Cettie.

John was naturally very mature, having been given many responsibilities at a young age. He had a ledger and kept track of the family's expenses, from charity to groceries. Whenever he and his family attended church, his mother would tell him and his siblings to put some money in the donation container.

Rockefeller was raised on the teachings of the Baptist church. It was a strict and pious upbringing. He was an ardent believer and very strict about working, giving, and staying pure.

He never drank and always worried that his father's nature would cause him to be like him.

Rockefeller was able to go to school and then to high school, but when it came time for him to go to college, William forbade any further education. John then tried to find a job, not wanting to have to rely on his father.

For six months, he would rise in the morning and spend the better part of the day walking around town looking for a job. It was summer, and the heat was so bad that he hurt his feet, and anyone in his shoes would have given up after the first two weeks, but John pressed on and kept searching.

Finally, he walked into the firm of Hewitt and Tuttle, a small business that acted as a brokerage firm for food. Since Rockefeller was good with numbers and accounts, he proved his ability during a brief interview. It so happened that the small firm needed someone to manage the books. It was a simple job, and Rockefeller had all the skills they needed to do the work. He could write, he could count, and, more importantly, he understood how to record ledgers. He got the job. He was asked to return after lunch and start right away. Rockefeller calmly walked out of the office after the interview but could not contain himself for long and gleefully skipped down the road. This habit of skipping persisted even in his old age whenever something went his way.

He was first paid $16 a month for three months. He did his job so well that his salary was raised to $31, then to $50, and then to $58 a month. Back then, it was a lot of money for a teenager.

In 1857, Tuttle, one of the partners of the firm, left the business, and Rockefeller was promoted to the position of chief bookkeeper. Tuttle had handled a large part of the accounts, and Rockefeller had been reporting to him and knew his job well. Even though Tuttle was paid $2,000 for his work, Rockefeller was only paid $500. Even at just a quarter of the former's salary, however, Rockefeller didn't complain but instead thought of ways to make his small fortune do more.

He received a raise the following year, and his salary increased to $600 a year.

It's amazing what a little money can do when your mind is clear and racing, and you're ambitious. Instead of splashing his newfound freedom, Rockefeller started investing his money and frugally saving the rest. He traded in the business of ham, flour, and pork and was able to make more money from it. As time passed, the company was not increasing his salary in a way that he expected, and, although he accepted it at first, in time he felt he was not getting his fair share and was being taken advantage of.

Rockefeller later approached Hewitt, the remaining partner, and asked for a raise. He wanted $800. Hewitt said that his maximum salary could only be $700. It turned out that Hewitt was not doing well, and even at $700 the firm was being stretched.

As Rockefeller listened to the plight of the company, he understood that the company was not in good shape and had an uncertain future. He also knew that William had recently invested $1,000 in the company. Rockefeller sought out his father and conveyed the message to him.

William marched straight over to Hewitt's office and demanded repayment of his investment.

In his later years, Rockefeller admitted that he would not have left Hewitt's firm had he been given the salary he wanted. Many additional factors caused Rockefeller to leave the firm, but it was driven primarily by his need to stretch his wings, and he seized the opportunity of Hewitt's downfall and that he had set aside a substantial amount of money from his salary and investments.

One thing that distinguished Rockefeller from his peers in Cleveland and beyond was that he was never satisfied with the status quo. He was inherently the sort of person who will always try to do better. In his advice to the younger generation, gleaned from his writings and from stories about him, he was always consistent in his stand that it was his duty to move ahead. It was almost a religious calling to do more.

Although he may have seemed the sensitive sort, he was also pragmatic and did not hesitate to swallow his pride. If he had to ask someone for money, he would, but he always paid it back. He learned this from his father. William once loaned his son some money but demanded interest on it. Rockefeller didn't hesitate to pay interest to his own father but took note of it in his heart.

Rockefeller finally left Hewitt's firm in early 1858. At this time, he was neighbors with Maurice B. Clark, a twenty-eight-year-old Englishman with an honest appreciation for Rockefeller's skills and ability, who once said that Rockefeller had "the reputation of being a young bookkeeper of more than ordinary ability and reliability." Rockefeller's reputation had preceded him. He was known as someone who was diligent, trustworthy, and bright.

Clark was working at the firm of Otis, Brownell at the time, and after Rockefeller left Hewitt, Clark approached him with the idea of the two of them setting up a company that bought and sold food on commission. He said that he and Rockefeller should each put $2,000 into the company. In 1858, this was equivalent to $61,276.34 today.

Unfortunately, Rockefeller had only $800 to spare. He did not know how he was supposed to gather together the necessary funds. He approached William for the loan. William told him that he had made plans to give $1,000 to all his children but at a 10 percent interest rate. Knowing better than to argue with his father to not have an interest rate, Rockefeller accepted the loan.

On April 1, 1858, he and Maurice formed the company and established an office at 32 River Street. Rockefeller was just under eighteen years old and already a partner and cofounder of a firm—a prestigious position for someone his age.

Rockefeller remarked, "It was a great thing to be my own employer. Mentally, I swelled with pride—a partner in a firm with $4,000 capital!"

Rockefeller took this partnership very seriously, and after the first day of work at the newly founded firm, he went back home on Cheshire Street and kneeling down begged God to bless his business.

Rockefeller never looked unfavorably upon his time at the firm of Hewitt and Tuttle. He cherished it as his first leap into business. When Rockefeller was ninety-five years old in 1934, he said to one of his grandsons, "Oh how blessed the young men are who have to struggle for a foundation and a beginning in life. I shall never cease to be grateful for three and a half years of apprenticeship and the difficulties to be overcome, all the way along."

Rockefeller was basically saying that anyone who has to crawl through the mud and dirt to be successful is better off than one who floats right into it. He was also expressing how he felt about his time at the firm, feeling it to be most important indeed.

When Clark and Rockefeller was established, they were well-liked, and the local newspaper, the *Cleveland Leader*, wrote, "As experienced, responsible and prompt businessmen, we recommend their house to the favorable consideration of our readers."

The business actually did well. At the time, there was a large demand for food products, including grain and meat. Companies in the produce industry would come to Clark and Rockefeller and ask them to sell it for them, and they would earn money based on commission.

Two months after its founding, a frost adversely affected Midwestern farms. Clark and Rockefeller had already ordered a shipment of beans, but when they arrived, they were partially spoiled and covered in dirt and gunk. They had to separate the good beans from the bad ones. Rockefeller recalled, "When we were not needed in the office, we used to go out to the warehouse, my partner and I, and sort out those beans."

Although this weather problem caused the firm to not do too well at the time, they still did well in the long run. By the end of that year, their company was worth $4,400.

Despite this success, however, the issue with the beans caused Rockefeller to ask his father for another loan, but William was not agreeable. He always found it amusing to play games with his son regarding money. He once said, "I trade with the boys and skin 'em, and I just beat 'em every time I can. I want to make 'em sharp."

At this time, Rockefeller was already used to how he and his father dealt with each other. In fact, he even softened his father's antics with positivity, saying, "To my father I owe a great debt in that he himself trained me to practical ways. He was engaged in different enterprises; he used to tell me about these things, explaining their significance; and he taught me the principles and methods of business."

Rockefeller's financial relationship with his father was most frustrating indeed. William would ask for the money he loaned to be returned to him at the worst possible moment when Rockefeller was not in a position to return the money. He said to Rockefeller, "My son, I find I have got to have that money." Rockefeller would reply, "Of course, you shall have it at once."

Rockefeller said that he knew his father was testing him, perhaps seeing whether or not he could repay his debt. He further said that after giving the money back to his father he would not use it for anything and would later have it available for lending. Rockefeller also said, "He would never know how angry I felt beneath the surface." That shows Rockefeller was actually incensed by his father's attitude but simply masked his anger with his expressionless face.

On the first anniversary after Clark and Rockefeller was founded, on April 1, 1859, a certain George W. Gardner, who had previously worked with Clark at Otis, Brownell, entered the picture. He was from a particularly well-to-do family and would go on to become the commodore of the Cleveland Yacht Club and mayor of Cleveland.

When Gardner joined Clark and Rockefeller, Rockefeller's name was scratched off, and the firm was reincorporated as Clark, Gardner and Company. Rockefeller was understandably upset about this but did not voice his anger. He said, "Maurice Clark was very pleasant about it." He went on to say, "And he said, 'Never mind. It won't be very long—before many years you'll be doing better than any of us.' Yes, he was very nice about it. I made no objection."

Much later, Rockefeller admitted that it was indeed a great pain to him, and he said, "I considered this a great injustice to me, as I was an equal partner, and Gardner brought in only his share of the capital, but I thought it best to submit."

Rockefeller was the kind of person who thought it was not nice or right to show his anger or his hurt, which were totally justifiable. Rockefeller did not gel with Clark and Gardner. He worked very hard and was very serious about his work. He would tell himself, "Your future hands on every day that passes." Many years before Rockefeller turned twenty-one years old, he was already being addressed as "Mr. Rockefeller."

Rockefeller was always very diligent about his work and only really happy when he secured a deal that was successful. He absolutely despised the attitude of his partners. They were much more relaxed and much less zealous than he was with their work. Gardner and Clark found Rockefeller to be both favorable and unpleasant. He was both a success and a stony-faced, unsmiling person. Do not take it for granted, though, that he was unhappy.

Rockefeller was afraid that if the business was not treated seriously they might have problems getting loans in the future. Thus, he made it a point to reduce their extravagances, keep their books tidy, and make sure they conducted themselves with dignity and integrity, which paid off in the long run.

Rockefeller learned early, thanks in no small part to his father, that bankability was an important issue. He was certain that one must conduct himself with integrity and honor so that in the event they needed to rely on their reputation they would be able to.

When Gardner and three of his friends bought a yacht for $2,000, Rockefeller showed extreme disapproval. It went against his character to splurge and waste on excesses, especially while the business was still expanding. It was always his style to invest the profits in the expansion of the company and then reap more profits. He was always focused on expansion. Spending money on a yacht was not his cup of tea.

Rockefeller often worked Saturdays (but not Sundays to observe the holy day), and on one

Saturday afternoon, while Rockefeller was deep in the books, Gardner approached him with a proposition, saying, "John, a little crowd of us are going to stake a sail over to Put-in-Bay, and I'd like to have you go along. I think it would do you good to get away from the office and get your mind off business for a while."

Rockefeller was particularly upset by this proposition, and Gardner would later say that Rockefeller responded most unkindly. Rockefeller said, "George Gardner, you're the most extravagant young man I ever knew! The idea of a young man like you, just getting a start in life, owning an interest in a yacht! You're injuring your credit at the banks—your credit and mine. . . . No, I won't go on your yacht. I don't even want to see it!"

Not only did the thought of not working on a Saturday offend Rockefeller, but he was also infuriated that money was being spent on extravagance and would damage their reputation with the banks.

He returned to his work, and Gardner said, "I see that there are certain things on which you and I probably will never agree. I think you like money better than anything else in the whole world, and I do not. I like to have a little fun along with business as I go through life."

If you are thinking that Rockefeller had an explosive temper and belted out his statement in anger, you would be wrong. He said what he had to say in the calmest of tones and in the most polite way possible.

Rockefeller continuously trained himself to mask his shaky feelings with a calm facade, but in his early days while still at Clark, Gardner and Company, he was not very good at it. Eventually, his Stoic nature earned him a favorable reputation wherever he went. The combination of his Stoic nature and abhorrence of wasting money worked hand in hand most of the time except for a few occasions. Clark, Gardner and Company once bet all of the firm's money on a rather sizeable shipment of grain to Buffalo. Rockefeller told his partners not to pay for the insurance and to simply keep the $150 that they would pay for the premium. Clark and

Gardner agreed to Rockefeller's idea but were not entirely comfortable with it.

Later that night, a violent storm occurred over Lake Erie. Rockefeller was found pacing in the office the next morning. He was extremely worried. When Gardner arrived, Rockefeller said to him, "Let's take out insurance right away." He went on to say, "We still have time—if the boat hasn't been wrecked by now." Gardner then paid the premium.

When Gardner returned to the office, a telegram in Rockefeller's hand informed them that the ship was safe and sound at its destination. That day Rockefeller returned home feeling sick to his stomach. This was caused by having paid $150 for nothing!

Gardner and Rockefeller were not the best of friends, but they spoke when needed and kept their distance at other times. Gardner had, however, developed a sort of liking for Rockefeller's father. Gardner said Rockefeller's father was ". . . one of the most companionable and most likeable old men I ever knew. He would crack jokes and have more to say in one conversation than John would utter in a week."

When Gardner asked Rockefeller about his father, John did not reply. He had no intention to speak ill of his father but also had no intention to lie. He didn't have much good to say and so decided that silence was best. With Clark, Gardner and Company expanding to Philadelphia, Gardner thought about meeting William, who was in Philadelphia. To do so, he spoke to Rockefeller and inquired about his father's address. Rockefeller feigned memory loss.

Gardner did not understand it. He knew Rockefeller had a very good memory but asked if he could get the address from Rockefeller's mother at lunchtime. Lunch came and went, but Rockefeller did not make any effort to talk about the matter. When they were later ready to leave the office for the day, Gardner asked Rockefeller for the address. Rockefeller went red and said he had forgotten to ask what the address was when he got home. Gardner did not pester him anymore, and he was thus never able to find out where William resided.

Gardner also observed how Rockefeller's father would come to the office and take out a large amount of money. Gardner said, "I wondered what business a man could be in that he would have $1,000 to spare one month and need it the next."

One of the reasons why Rockefeller had been unwilling to talk about his father or his whereabouts was mainly because of his father's double life. As William had two families in different locations, Rockefeller wasn't going to talk about it. When Rockefeller began to understand the gravity of William's two marriages, he was, on the inside, extremely taken aback. He did, however, hide his shakiness with a very calm outlook.

Rockefeller was always very serious about his work. While he took care of the accounts and the firm's books, Clark took care of what the firm did—purchasing and selling goods. Rockefeller was always the first to arrive at work and the last to leave. He was always very meticulous and looking for mistakes. Clark recalled that Rockefeller was a nice person, but he was ". . . too exact. He was methodical to an extreme, careful as to details and exacting to a fraction. If there was a cent due us, he wanted it. If there was a cent due a customer, he wanted the customer to have it."

As with most successful men, Rockefeller was often forced to battle his own pride, as when a bank once rejected his loan application he swore to himself that he would one day be the richest man in the world.

Every time he would have those thoughts he would tell himself what his mother had told him when he was young, "Pride goes before a fall." Every night when he lay down he would remind himself with a mantra that guided him "Because you have got a start, you think you are quite a merchant; look out, or you will lose your head— go steady. Are you going to let this money puff you up? Keep your eyes open. Don't lose your balance." He was basically telling himself not to be distracted by money, and by telling himself this every night, it was pounded into his head.

While trying to expand the business, Rockefeller travelled across both Indiana and Ohio. He met with people and proposed that they come to his firm. Although most people believed that Rockefeller was a cold person who plucked clients from other firms and forcefully placed them with his own, he was in fact very gentle and calm in the way he operated. He was driven and focused, which sometimes rubbed others against their grain.

Rockefeller would meet with someone, say that he thought his associates in business were up to par, say he hoped he wasn't an intrusion for him, and then say that he had something to offer that he "believed" would be of benefit to the person he was talking to. He would say that he did not expect an answer right away but gave the person time to think about the offer and that he would come back to talk over the matter once more.

Orders for buying and selling goods began to pile up. Rockefeller said, "I found that old men had confidence in me right away, and after I stayed a few weeks in the country, I returned home and the consignments came in and our business was increased and it opened up a new world for me."

Rockefeller was skilled in handling people well. He was a very determined and persevering person. He would overcome whatever he needed to in order to achieve what he envisioned. When he went on sales trips and business started to flow in, he found that he had another problem— not enough carriages to carry all the goods.

One time a customer of Clark, Gardner and Company wanted to pay the firm for their services before receiving the goods he wanted. This customer was a very lucrative customer, and doing such a thing would go against certain business policies. Rockefeller turned down the offer and tried to keep his customer. Rockefeller recalled, "But he stormed about, and in the end I had the further humiliation of confessing to my partner that I had failed."

Rockefeller would later find out that the reason why the customer was so headstrong about carrying out his proposition was that it was actually a trap laid by a banker in the area. The banker was testing whether or not Rockefeller and his partners would be able to hold back from taking the easy route and adhere to their ethics.

Although Rockefeller did not trust bankers, they were crucial for his success. Rockefeller said, "The hardest problem all through my business career was to obtain enough capital to do all the business I wanted to do and could do, given the necessary amount of money."

Banks that were established on Main Street were not really financially strong, and not many people were confident enough to be customers of the banks. Clark, Gardner and Company kept money in a safe that would be used as backup.

The first time Rockefeller received a loan from someone other than his father he borrowed $2,000 from Truman P. Handy, an old and kind banker. Rockefeller felt a certain sense of happiness. He said to himself as he walked, "Just think of it. A bank had trusted me for $2,000! I felt that I was now a man of importance in the community."

When Handy loaned Rockefeller the money, he made him take an oath that he would not use the money for speculative purposes. Handy became an important guide for Rockefeller, who knew that his character dictated his credit rating. What made banks comfortable with Rockefeller was that he was a cornerstone of the Baptist Mission Church on Erie Street.

When Rockefeller was older, he was against borrowing money but was very willing to do it when he needed it. Maurice B. Clark remarked, "Oh, John was the greatest borrower you ever saw!" Just like William, Rockefeller knew how to manipulate the masses to satisfy his needs. If Rockefeller wished to borrow $5,000, he would spread a rumor among the people that he was going to invest $10,000. This would consolidate the credit of the company he was working in and make banks have a reason to lend him money.

The Civil War was a good time for Rockefeller and his firm. Produce companies were able to make a lot of money by supplying food to the Union troops, and Rockefeller was one of them.

Rockefeller viewed the Civil War as a time to make money and hired people to take his place. He supported the North and was very strong in his views about ending slavery. Even as a young boy in school, he wanted slavery abolished. In one of the essays he wrote about freedom in school, he said that the slave owners, whom he called "cruel masters," made their slaves work "beneath the scorching suns of the South. How under such circumstances can America call herself free?"

Before entering his twenties, Rockefeller was donating money to causes that helped African-Americans. During this time, most of the people in Cleveland were against slavery, and it did not exist there. The Underground Railroad was an institution that transported black slaves who had run from their masters to free states and Canada, where they could be free. In Cleveland, blacks would also discreetly board ships not very far from Rockefeller's office.

When slave hunters came looking for slaves near Cleveland, those who stood for the eradication of slavery would hastily go to the Public Square where the Stone Church stood and ring the bell, which served as a warning to Clevelanders.

In the 1860 presidential elections, Rockefeller voted for Abraham Lincoln. On the day before the Civil War began, Rockefeller went to certain gatherings where all the attendees voiced their strong condemnation of slavery. Evangelicals were particularly opposed to slavery as were Baptists, who treated blacks cordially and allowed them to speak in their churches about ending slavery.

The first battle of the Civil War was a Confederate victory when they captured Fort Sumter. In turn, President Abraham Lincoln called for seventy-five thousand people to enlist in the Union army. Rockefeller, however, did not join. He said, "I wanted to go in the army and do my part . . . But it was simply out of the question. We were in a new business, and if I had not stayed it must have stopped—and with so many dependent on it."

Rockefeller's decision to stay at the firm because he thought it would fail was perhaps because his father had left him and his family. He felt he needed to stay and do his duty in this situation. Rockefeller was a complex person with many opposing forces tugging at him from all sides. On the one hand, he took filial duty seriously, and he afforded his father the respect and deference that was due, but it is hard to find evidence that he showed any love in any way. In his younger days when he had yet to form a mind of his own, Rockefeller loved his father and looked forward to being with him. He also enjoyed those times when his father would return after weeks of being gone with money and gifts for everyone. After managing on a shoestring budget with his mother and siblings, the abundance of money and gifts along with the return of his father softened his heart, and he associated his father's presence with happiness and comfort. That, however, did not last long, as William's unorthodox ways and mean streak soon forced Rockefeller to feel very uncomfortable around him. It was hard for Rockefeller to feel warm and fuzzy when his own father would charge him rent for living in his house, charge interest on money he borrowed, and asked for loans to be repaid at a moment's notice.

Chapter 2 The Civil War

"Don't be afraid to give up the good to acquire
the great."

— **John D. Rockefeller**

During the Civil War, the U.S. government
needed all citizens on deck to help with the war
effort by joining the military. They did, however,
allow people who provided for or supported
their family, whether it was their brothers and
sisters, their mother and father, or their own
children, to not enlist. Rockefeller was among
those who were the sole providers of their
family. Although Rockefeller was only twenty-
one years old, he acted as a father for his siblings
and took care of a sizeable family with six
members, excluding him—his mother, sisters—
Mary Ann Rockefeller and Lucy Rockefeller
Briggs; and brothers, Frank, William, and

Francis Rockefeller. Frank was the only one who would eventually join the Union Army.

Rockefeller was an ardent supporter of the North and not only gave to the cause but also supported the soldiers. One day a Captain Levi Scofield, one of Rockefeller's friends, entered his firm's office with thirty soldiers who had just joined the army. Rockefeller took money from his safe and handed out $10 to each of them, a total of $300! One of the soldiers said, "God, but he must be rich." Another soldier said, "Yes, they say he is a rich man—that he is worth $10,000!"

By this time, people were beginning to believe that Rockefeller was a wealthy man. The year before the Civil War ended Rockefeller was giving $300 a year to stand-ins in the army and the dependent families that relied on them. Furthermore, he was donating money to funds that helped the war.

After the Civil War began, he and Clark would always keep tabs on the conflict. They studied very detailed maps and tracked the progress of the war. Other people also came to their office to see as well. Rockefeller recalled, "Our office became a great rallying-place. We were all deeply interested. Men used to drop in often, and we followed the war keenly, reading the latest dispatches and studying the maps."

Frank, the only Rockefeller brother to join the army, was very much like his father. He could be friendly one moment and then become easily agitated. Frank was sixteen when he wanted to join, but Rockefeller would not let him. When Frank approached him and asked for $75 to join the army, Rockefeller refused to give him the money. According to George Gardner, Rockefeller actually lectured him, saying, "You would be a wild, foolish boy to go away and waste youthful years that you might utilize in getting a start and making money."

In the end, it was Gardner who loaned Frank the $75. This loan was the first of a great many that Frank would get but not repay. Gardner's going against what Rockefeller wanted and helping Frank join the army would cause their already shaky relationship to fray even more.

Before receiving the money to join the army, Frank had actually tried some deceitful tactics to do so. William scolded him, however, for not being open about his wishes and plans. He said to him, "Young man, when you go to war you will say goodbye to the family and go out the front door in broad daylight." William of all people was condemning secrecy. It was quite ironic that a man who lied so often and had hundreds of skeletons in his closet could speak against secrecy.

To join the army, Frank decided to pose as older than he was, and to not lie, he wrote the number eighteen on the sole of his shoe. So, when the recruiting officer asked him his age, Frank said, "I'm over eighteen, sir."

After some time, Rockefeller simply gave up trying to stop his brother from going to war and funded him by paying for all his necessary equipment, such as his gun and clothes, during the three years that Frank fought in the war.

Frank was a soldier of the Seventh Ohio Volunteer Infantry. During the Civil War, he was injured twice, once at Cedar Mountain and again at Chancellorsville. Frank was deeply upset that his brother was nice and comfortable and making lots of money while he was fighting and being injured.

The North was able to greatly advance its economy during the Civil War. The country developed in such a way so as to meet the demands of war, and the railroads, iron mills, and other industries became more efficient. For instance, more sophisticated technology aided the war, such as reapers and sewing machines. The reapers harvested produce that eventually became food for the soldiers, and the sewing machines were used to make their uniforms.

To make progress, the U.S. government issued land grants, which affected Rockefeller's early life. Because more railroads were being built, Rockefeller was able to pay less to transport his goods by pitting two different railroads against each other to his advantage.

Since industry was booming during the Civil War, many people turned their backs on their simple farms and set their sights on becoming rich. It was a mini agricultural and industrial revolution fueled by the ongoing war.

Although Rockefeller's firm did not get any substantially profitable jobs from the government, they were able to make money from the increased prices of goods. Their company bought and sold things that consumers needed and had large quantities of products in their warehouses. In 1863, an advertisement of Rockefeller's company showed the quantity and quality of their inventory. They stored more than two hundred barrels of pork, more than five hundred bushels of clover seed, thirteen hundred barrels of salt, and eight hundred bushels of timothy seed.

As their business grew partly because of the increasing transportation infrastructure in the form of railroads and because the war was still going on, the profits of the company increased, and the other partners saw fit to spend and live lavishly.

For Rockefeller, aside from his support of the war effort and looking after his family, he was more interested in expanding his business. He had built a reputation of being rich, which led him to think he controlled the banks and could go to them at any time and request a loan for a particular project. By this point in his life, Rockefeller's company owned four warehouses, all of which were on River Street.

As the profits rose and the difference between Gardner and Rockefeller grew more stark, the time eventually came for Rockefeller to get rid of him. Not only did he decide to show Gardner the exit, but he also made it a point to remove him from all accounts of his journal. It was some time in 1862 that Rockefeller severed the relationship.

Chapter 3 Titusville

"When people think of the oil industry, they think of Rockefeller, much like when people think of the software industry, they think of Bill Gates."

— H.W. Brands

The Civil War made Rockefeller quite a rich man. This wealth, however, in retrospect, was incomparable to the wealth he obtained from the oil business.

Even before crude oil was harvested by Edwin Drake in Titusville, it was already coming out of the ground. It seeped into Oil Creek, mixing with the water. Oil was prevalent in many places, including salt wells and water wells, contaminating the water. You could see it flowing in creeks and streams. In the beginning, it was more of a nuisance than a blessing. It was dirty, toxic, and difficult to clean. It would nonetheless soon be considered black gold.

Seneca natives had a variety of uses for the oil. They used it to paint themselves when going to war, and they used it as medicine albeit ineffectively as well as a disinfectant for the skin. The Indians harvested the oil by placing blankets or pieces of fabric in the running water in the creek and let them soak up the oil. The Indians then took the blankets and dried them in the sun to let the water evaporate from the cloth. Once the water was gone and the heavier oil remained, they squeezed out the oil.

Around 1850, one Samuel Kier collected the oil in the salt wells that his father owned and bottled it. They were half-pints, and Samuel sold the oil, calling it Kier's Rock Oil as a medicine. It was supposed to cure bronchitis and liver problems. Of course, it didn't.

Oil was soon used in communities around the country. It was used to light lamps, but whale oil was primarily used for this purpose at the time. Whale blubber was shipped throughout the country, but whalers were not able to keep up with the demand, which made it expensive, and only the wealthy could afford such luxuries and light their homes at night. The rest of the people, such as farmers and villagers and the poor in the city, were forced to go without light until morning.

Although there were other ways of lighting their homes with tallow (derived from animal) and coal oil (derived from shale), these were expensive as well, as the process of extraction and the supply of these oils were limited. Other forms of oil could also be used, which included cottonseed oil and lard oil, but these were not affordable or convenient to use. An alternative was necessary, and those who could solve the problem would be paid handsomely. Electricity and the light bulb were still a long way off.

Then along came George Bissell, who had graduated from Dartmouth College and had worked as a school principal, a professor of Greek language, a lawyer, and a journalist. In his spare time, he was also an inventor. Sometime in the 1850s, he had an idea for a new way to fuel the lights in people's homes. He thought that perhaps the oil struck in the western regions of Pennsylvania could be a better fuel for lamps.

Bissell then founded the Pennsylvania Rock Oil Company and sent a small amount of the oil found in the area to Benjamin Silliman Jr., a professor of chemistry at Yale University. In 1855, Silliman concluded that Bissell's suspicions were true. Rock oil could be processed to be a fuel for lamps.

Now that this was possible, the Pennsylvania Rock Oil Company faced a different problem. They had to gather large amounts of the oil. Practically no infrastructure existed for oil exploration at the time. All they had were streams and creeks that showed traces of this material, which looked like a contaminant rather than an asset. They decided that since it came from the ground they needed to look for underground deposits. Near the end of 1857, close to three years after Silliman corroborated Bissell's suspicions, explorers were commissioned to look for large deposits of oil. Today, there is a body of science in the field of exploration, which is a billion-dollar business, but back then it was anybody's guess. At this point, Bissell's company had been renamed the Seneca Oil Company in tribute to the Seneca tribe that had been wringing oil from blankets they soaked in the river.

It was thanks to a Mr. Townsend, a banker in New Haven who helped finance this exploration mission, that someone was able to search for large deposits of oil. He sent Edwin Drake, a man in his late thirties who suffered from a constant back problem. Drake was eventually given the title of Colonel and dispatched to Titusville, Pennsylvania, in December 1857.

At this time, Oil Creek Valley, situated in Titusville, was not very sophisticated or modern. It was still densely packed with thick forests of hemlock and pine trees and the usual wildlife. These were harsh conditions to search for oil when you consider the dense forest and the lack of expertise in finding something below ground. Pipe had to be brought in, and hauling all that equipment was not easy. The people of Oil Creek liked Drake but thought he was wasting his time.

They couldn't imagine there were any deposits of this toxic material.

He used the same methods to find oil that salt miners used in the salt mines. This was the first use of derricks to explore for oil. Back then the derricks were made of wood and towered ten to thirty feet above the ground, where they bored a hole in the earth.

Finally, after a long period of time, Drake succeeded in finding a well that contained this heavy, sludgelike material.

On Saturday, August 27, 1859, almost one and a half years after arriving in Oil Creek, Colonel Drake struck oil. It had now been conclusively proven that oil did exist in certain pockets below ground. Drake's method was viable and effective, and he now had a system that was replicable in the future, which was the key to future success.

His discovery made news, and before long there was a rush to settle in Titusville. More derricks were set up, and more holes were bored to tap that well. All they had was crude oil, though, and you couldn't do anything with it until it was refined.

The next sector of the oil industry that was developed was refining the toxic sludge. To process the crude oil, numerous refineries were set up by independent companies to process the oil that was coming from independent drillers.

In less than a year after Drake struck oil, a large number of refineries were set up in Oil Creek, but they could not extract usable heating oil to any profitable degree. Their methods were crude, and their output was low, but it was better than nothing. A lot of sludge was discarded in streams and in the ground after the refining process, but most of this discarded sludge still had usable hydrocarbons.

We can't say with any certainty what impression Rockefeller may have had when Edwin Drake began producing oil with his derrick, but we do have some insight into his view of oil itself based on what he wrote at the time. "These vast stores of wealth were the gifts of the great Creator, the bountiful gifts of the great Creator." Rockefeller also said, "Colonel Drake and the Standard Oil

Company and all others connected with this industry had the opportunity for useful work in preparing and distributing this valuable product to supply the wants of the world."

Even in the midst of commercial success and potential for profit, Rockefeller continued his pious and holy appreciation for the gifts of the earth that came from the Creator. That was his typical frame of mind. He was evidently very grateful to Colonel Edwin Drake and rightfully so. If it hadn't been for Drake, there might have been no way to harvest the oil, and the young oil industry would have bubbled into nothingness.

Because Rockefeller believed the Almighty had furnished the world with kerosene, it emboldened him and propelled him to do what he did and change the world the way he did. It was not all about money, as Ida Tarbell would come to conclude in her writings.

In the beginning, Rockefeller was not very enthusiastic about the young oil industry, and it took him some time to begin working at it full-time. It's possible that at the beginning of 1860 the firm of Clark and Rockefeller was charged with delivering a shipment of crude oil. Although Rockefeller was already in the business of oil (transporting it), he did not pay too much attention to it. In the end, it would be thanks to Samuel Andrews that Rockefeller would enter the oil industry in any meaningful way.

Chapter 4 Rockefeller Meets Oil

"I believe that thrift is essential to well-ordered living."

— John D. Rockefeller

Clark was friends with Samuel Andrews, being that they were both countrymen from Wiltshire in southwest England. Andrews was an ambitious mechanic, a skilled fixer of all things mechanical, and a self-taught chemist. He was congenial, with a bright red complexion and easily stood out in a crowd.

Andrews came to Cleveland in the 1850s and started working in a business owned by C.A. Dean, the owner of a lard oil refinery. During his time with Dean, he learned how to distill coal oil, tallow, and candles. In 1860, the first form of kerosene made from crude oil was developed. Andrews had refined this kerosene from a shipment of ten barrels of crude oil that came from Pennsylvania. Back then refining oil was done with sulfuric acid. Refining crude oil, however, was not common. Only a few people knew how to do it, but many were interested in it.

Andrews believed that kerosene would be the best lighting fuel to replace tallow or blubber. Unfortunately for him, however, he was not financially well off. He did not earn much money for his work, and his wife would sew for customers to make extra income, but two years after making kerosene from crude oil, Andrews began to think about quitting Dean's company. He began to look for people who would finance him and would often go to Clark and Rockefeller (company) in search of an investor.

Andrews and Rockefeller were not strangers. They had met at the Erie Street Baptist Mission Church and Andrews, his wife, and Rockefeller knew one another. Maurice B. Clark recalled how he responded to Andrews about his talk about refining oil. Clark said, "I told him there was no chance, that John and I together did not have more than $250 we could spare out of our business; we simply hadn't enough working capital, together with our credit at the banks, to enable us to make advances to our suppliers, paying insurance and rent." He was basically telling Andrews that they were very tight and could not spare much for his venture.

Andrews wasn't going to back down though. After having no success with Clark, he went to Rockefeller. By now, Rockefeller had already put his money in stock of a railroad, and he also had extra money. He was easier to approach. He was saving his money and investing his profits, not spending it as was the case with Clark. Rockefeller liked Andrews' plan and was willing to help him. Andrews then went back to Clark. At first, Clark just tried to push him away. Then Andrews said, "Mr. Rockefeller thinks well of it." Clark then said, "Well, if John will go in, I will."

Later, Rockefeller would paint himself as someone who was not very enthusiastic and not as interested as others were regarding the oil industry. He said that he was not very confident about the matter but was actually forced into the business by Andrews, Clark, and his two brothers.

In the end, Clark and Rockefeller invested $4,000 in Andrews' company. This amount was only half of what was needed. Andrews' company was called Andrews, Clark and Company. Rockefeller was now twenty-four years old and involved in the business that would make him the richest man in the world.

Because they initially thought the oil industry would not be as lucrative or successful as it turned out to be, Rockefeller and his partners did not pay much attention to it and kept it as a *second* business, something that was not their main line of work and a smaller part of their career.

Rockefeller was quite far from the oil fields of Pennsylvania. Like others who wanted to start a life in the oil industry but were far from the source, he was forced to go into the business of refining.

The location where Rockefeller chose to build Excelsior Works, his first refinery, was in a peaceful countryside more than a mile away from Cleveland. It was a sloping landscape. Kingsbury Run, a small, flowing body of water, was lined with red brick and cradled in serenity. The land where Rockefeller wanted to build his refinery featured grazing cows and towering trees. These were not seen as hindrances, though, and not long after railroads arrived in the area it turned into a bustling center of activity.

On Friday, November 3, 1863, an Atlantic and Great Western Railroad train arrived at a train station in Cleveland. It was nicely decorated and a harbinger of how Cleveland and New York City would be connected. It also allowed for a straightforward trip to the oil site in Pennsylvania.

Rockefeller was able to transport his goods both by waterway and land, and he was able to persuade the railroads to charge him reduced rates. He used the leverage of competition to knock down the price of transportation. He would pit one railroad operator against the other or the railroad against shipping companies to get a better rate. He was indeed a master negotiator.

Thus, during the rest of his life in the oil industry, he would always think very carefully about where he set up his refineries. The site of his refinery was a strategic location. The other refineries that he would establish would also be strategically placed.

Very soon after Rockefeller set up his refinery near Kingsbury Run, several other refineries followed suit. At the time, Cleveland had a population of 44,000 and was filled with young men who were desperately trying to succeed in life. It was really very easy to get into the business of refining oil. It cost less money to start a refinery and hire workers than to open a store. At the time, you could set up a refinery for $1,000 or less.

By the second half of 1863, twenty oil refineries were located in Cleveland, all of which exported 25 percent of the kerosene they distilled. In the beginning, everyone who ventured into the oil business was making lots of money. During the American Civil War, crude oil had many purposes, one of which was nursing injured Union soldiers, and it was also used as an alternative to turpentine that had originally come from the South.

It wasn't long before Rockefeller began to dislike Andrews. He criticized him, saying that he was deceptive and stubborn, which he attributed to his English roots. Their relationship was not always sour, though, and they were actually friendly to one another in the beginning.

The reporter Ida Tarbell, who would later cause the American government to prosecute Standard Oil, wrote nicely about Andrews, going against Rockefeller's judgment of him, saying that Andrews was "a mechanical genius." Tarbell credited him with bettering the standard of kerosene and increasing the amount of kerosene that was distilled from a barrel of oil.

When Rockefeller first entered the oil business, he was quite personally involved. It was only when he grew older that he would become more physically uninvolved. In the early days of Excelsior, Rockefeller would arrive at Kingsbury Run at 6:30 a.m. He would do what normal workers would do even though he owned the company. He would roll the barrels where they needed to go. He would do small tasks here and there and basically did not care that he was doing the work of a regular worker. He wanted to do what was necessary and didn't care that he was doing it himself.

Whenever oil was refined, a small portion of sulfuric acid would be left behind, and Rockefeller came up with a way to put this to use. He wanted to use it as a fertilizer, which was the first time that a waste product had been made into a useful commodity.

To put this into context, you have to realize that his family faced hard times when he was young, sometimes not knowing where the next meal was coming from. This sort of uncertainty and unstable environment drove him to be independent and self-sufficient to the point that he didn't wait for others to do the work. He would just jump in and get it done.

Whenever there were not enough barrels at the refinery, he resorted to constructing them himself. One time Rockefeller became quite upset with how a mistake was made in money owed to their plumber. He decided to take things into his own hands and told Andrews, "Hire a plumber by the month. Let us buy our own pipes, joints, and all other plumbing material."

In the end, contrary to what Rockefeller and his partners had thought in the beginning, the oil business that they conducted became more lucrative than their produce venture. Although the whole oil industry was prone to unexpected events, Rockefeller's refinery never suffered losses or bad years. It was well managed and well run, with foresight and diligence.

Rockefeller was the kind of person who always did what was needed to the best of his ability and to the fullest measure he could provide. There was no shortcuts and no half-baked efforts.

Rockefeller shared a room with William Rockefeller Jr. and would quite often wake him up in the middle of the night and talk about an idea for something and ask William what he thought of it. His brother would simply talk about it later and go back to sleep.

Rockefeller, Andrews, and Clark would often meet at his Cheshire Street home before the sun rose and discuss oil. Mary Ann Rockefeller, Rockefeller's sister, said that Clark and Andrews would always appeal to him. She said, "They did not seem to want to go without him. They would walk in and visit in the dining room while John was at breakfast. Mary Ann could not stand that they were constantly talking about oil. She just couldn't stand it. She said, "I got sick of it and wished morning after morning that they would talk of something else."

Rockefeller was very passionate about his oil business. He was also very passionate when it came to the church or more specifically the Baptist Church. Clark said that "John had abiding faith in two things—the Baptist creed and oil."

From a rather renowned historian's perspective, he was both "very mature and very young." He could be very serious and firm and also very jolly and merry. Rockefeller found happiness in his work and felt especially happy when he secured a profitable contract. One of the people who knew him during his early days said, "The only time I ever saw John Rockefeller enthusiastic was when a report came in from the creek that his buyer had secured a cargo of oil at a figure much below the market price. He bounded from his chair with a shout of joy, danced up and down, hugged me, threw up his hat, acted so like a madman that I have never forgotten it."

Because Rockefeller sometimes acted extremely merry, it made his usual silence and expressionless face more pronounced. Perhaps it showed that he was actually a happy man or that only very few things made him happy, and that the rest of the time he was not.

Part of the reason why Rockefeller was able to achieve dominance in the oil industry was because it was still an unstable industry in the beginning. He took something that was risky and identified the risk that would bankrupt a producer or a refiner and realized that the only way to beat the odds was to grow large and do it with the assistance of numerous participants. That meant that instead of building everything from scratch Rockefeller used the strategy of acquisitions to grow his company and mitigate the risk of competitive forces.

According to Rockefeller's enemies, he was an evil spirit or something that caused people to be afraid. This first occurred along Oil Creek, which is known as the Oil Regions. The Oil Regions surrounded Oil City, Titusville, and Franklin.

Before Excelsior Works was set up, Rockefeller traveled to Titusville. The journey required him to travel by train and then in a stagecoach through the dense forests that lined Oil Creek. He did not like the journey and often showed his displeasure. Many other people also wanted to go to Oil Creek, and the aisles in between the seats of the train were jammed with people, and many more sat on the roof of the carriages. Anyone who was delicate or nervous would have died in those situations.

One of the difficulties in getting the oil to the train was the terrain that existed between the derricks and the station. For the oil to get from Oil Creek to the trains, it had to be transported over twenty miles of undulating terrain. Some men were hired to move them, and they charged quite a preposterous sum for their services—up to $3 or $4 per barrel.

In 1861, $3 was a lot of money—worth about $85 today. In their defense, though, they did have to do a lot of work, transporting forty-two gallon barrels for more than twenty miles over difficult terrain. Each barrel weighed approximately 134 kilos. In volume, that same barrel carried forty-two gallons of oil. It has since been known as a Pennsylvania barrel, and that measurement is still used today.

During the transportation of oil, some of the barrels would fall to the ground, break, and spill their contents. It wasn't long until the landscape was soaked with this toxic and corrosive sludge.

The workers eventually started to use horses to pull the barrels, and these horses would sometimes get stuck in the mud if it rained, and sludge would line the path from the derricks to the station. Extra horses sometimes had to be used just to pull out the horses that got stuck in the mud.

These horses that were used to pull the barrels of oil encountered much difficulty and were whipped incessantly until many of them just dropped dead. Their carcasses were left to decompose and be broken down by the extremely corrosive crude oil.

Oil was also transported across the Allegheny River in two ways—either loaded on flatbed steamers or the barrels would be flushed down the river to their destination.

To do this, the barrels were placed on barges, and temporary dams and floodgates were used to hold back the water. When a sufficient amount of water was behind the dam, the gates would be released, and the rush of water would then push the barrels downstream to Pittsburgh.

Rockefeller recounted that "Lots of oil was lost by the capsizing of barges and smashing of barrels in the confusion and crush of the rafts." In 1863, the Allegheny River was filled with so much toxic crude oil that the river caught fire. A bridge in Franklin even burned down.

Rockefeller saw that the once peaceful and serene countryside had been turned into a black landscape where the oil industry now blossomed. The area was filled with shacks, derricks, engine houses, and tanks. It was all messy and filthy. Rockefeller observed that the oil industry was filled with people and groups of people who entered the industry and then quickly left it. He said, "You will remember that the business in its early years was a sort of gold-field rush." He also said, "Great fortunes were made by some of the first adventurers, and everything was carried on in a sort of capitalist development, when the colorful daredevils and pioneering speculators give way, as Max Weber wrote, to the 'men who had grown up in the hard school of life, calculating and daring at the same time, above all temperate and reliable, shrewd and completely devoted to their business, with strictly bourgeois opinions and principles.'"

When Rockefeller visited the Oil Regions, the oil industry no longer seemed that it would soon fade into nothingness. Oil was not a passing fad. It was here to stay, and in late 1861 the Empire

Well was built, one of the largest at that time. It was owned by two people from Cleveland and produced three thousand barrels a day.

The Empire Well produced so much oil that it came spewing out at such a rapid rate that the owners of the well could not find a way to harvest all the oil and were not given enough time to even acquire barrels to collect the oil. Normal people would rush over with all sorts of containers, from cups to buckets, to collect the precious oil.

Due to the rapid rise in the production of crude oil, the selling price plummeted. It fell to ten cents per barrel, yet they had to pay workers $3 to $4 per barrel just to transport it to the train station. Producers were suddenly losing money.

During the early stages of the oil industry, there were always violent changes in the dynamic. Either lots of oil would be available and prices would plunge, or there would be so little oil that prices would dramatically increase. When this happened, people would wonder if the supply of oil was running out.

When the oil industry first began, people were always afraid that the oil supply would deplete. An associate of Andrew Carnegie once came up with the idea of pooling oil by digging a large area in the ground and storing barrels of oil inside it so that when the oil supply ran out they could sell that collection of oil and make a nice profit. That started the first known event of oil price manipulation by the restriction of supply. We see it happening today with OPEC producers restricting production.

Many stories have been told about Rockefeller's first trip to the Pennsylvanian oil fields, but one story told by Franklin Breed is rather noteworthy. To get to Breed's oil well, the two men rode on horses, but they walked the last half mile on foot. At one point, they had to cross a small body of water that was about four feet deep and five or six feet wide. In the body of water was sediment that had been removed from the bottom of tanks. It looked like tar, sitting in the water, mixed with the mud. Over the wide body of water was a log measuring six inches in length. Breed always crossed over it, and it was like second nature to him. Rockefeller, however, was not so used to walking over logs and said he wasn't going to, but he tried and fell into the water. After falling, he looked at Breed, a smile on his face, and said, "Well, Breed, you have got me into the oil business head and ears."

Rockefeller probably looked very reserved and aloof to the workers who drilled the wells, but in truth, he said that he actually liked being among them and said they were ". . . pleasant fellows, the same type we meet in the mining regions— jolly, good-natured, the happy-go-lucky sort." Although Rockefeller was not totally cordial when he said this, he did not brush off the workers or anyone for that matter. He would always listen to what they had to say and collect all the information that he could gather. He would then repeat all the important parts to himself until they were etched in his memory. In doing this, he respected even the fool's opinion, which only a very small number of people are able to bring themselves to do. Too many are filled with too much pride to listen to even the worker, but Rockefeller, in his quest for knowledge, listened to everyone regardless of their position or status.

Rockefeller once said, "It is very important to remember what other people tell you, not so much what you yourself already know." Although the place where oil originated in the United States enabled Rockefeller to amass his unfathomable wealth and power, he did not like the area. It was filled with immoral people, gambling and indulging in pleasures of the flesh. The more that Rockefeller went to Oil Creek and the Oil Regions, the more his character hardened against immorality. Due to his passionate feeling about not drinking, he felt most upset when he was around people who drank. It has been suspected that that was a reason why he very rarely went to Oil Creek and the Regions.

At first, the oil business was not treated as an industry. Everyone was uncertain whether or not the oil frenzy and the entire oil business would just suddenly evaporate or if it would last and continue to do good for people. Most oil miners would quickly remove all the oil in their field. At the time, certain miners would not drill straight but in a diagonal direction so as to harvest another miner's oil.

What differentiated Rockefeller from his fellow adventurers in the oil business, aside from his unrelenting character, is that he eventually came to believe that the oil business would not fizzle out. He believed that it would be a long-lasting affair. It was because of this belief that he was able to succeed as he did.

If you look at this psychologically, you could perhaps say that those who thought the oil business would eventually fizzle away treated it very carelessly. Rockefeller, rightfully thinking that the oil industry would continue, devoted his time and care to the business, which allowed *his* business to thrive.

It was wise for Rockefeller to go into the business of oil refining. An oil miner did not enjoy as much success as a refiner because it was more difficult. To harvest oil, you had to land on a site with oil below the land. Mining oil was much more risky than refining. Being a refiner, you could trust that you would always have business, as some miner or another person would always come to you to process his oil, and you were safe.

Very soon after entering the oil business, Rockefeller understood that he could have more control over the oil industry as a refiner. As it would turn out, his company, Standard Oil, would be the largest oil refining company in the world until its breakup in 1911.

Rockefeller was always able to know who would hinder or help him in his business. He never liked to be treated inferiorly even by those who held a higher position than he did. Whenever he sensed that someone was treating him as less than an equal, he would stop it at once.

Clark's brother had joined the firm, and Rockefeller came to hate him as much as he did Clark and Rockefeller's former partner George W. Gardner. They were too lavish in their ways, and Rockefeller absolutely despised them for it. Rockefeller always minded his own business, did his work, and crunched the numbers, and it was because of this that he was seen by his partners as less of a man than he was. He would spend time thinking about how he could get rid of the Clark brothers, and they would not even see the final blow coming.

Rockefeller was always very meticulous and very careful with all the books, and the elder Clark thought this was all Rockefeller could do . . . that he had no imagination or spirit and was just a cold calculator. Rockefeller said, "He did not think I could do anything but keep accounts and look after the finances." Rockefeller also said, "You see, it took him a long time to see that I was no longer a boy."

Rockefeller believed that Clark was jealous of him because he was successful, which went against Clark's belief that Rockefeller was dispensable. In the beginning, Rockefeller just kept his anger toward Clark within him and said nothing. While he and Rockefeller were talking about business, Clark would often say, "What in the world would you have done without me?" Rockefeller said that he ". . . bore it in silence. It does no good to dispute with such a man."

One thing that was very clear at least in Rockefeller's mind was that he was the one bringing in the money and for the better part making what should've perhaps been his *own* company successful. As Rockefeller said, "I was the one who made the firm's success. I kept the books, looked out for the money."

Rockefeller was naturally very silent and reserved and thus did not warn his partners about his plan. He thought it best to throw it at them when they had no idea it was coming.

After having entered the oil business, Clark's brother, James Clark, joined the business. Rockefeller would grow to absolutely despise James, who was also a prizefighter. James was a bully who liked to trample on those around him. He attempted to make Rockefeller cower, but he failed. Rockefeller was always strong and fearless and was not affected by James' snobbishness and extreme rudeness. One day James stormed into Rockefeller's office and began to swear, scream, and shout at him. In response, Rockefeller simply sat in his chair, rested his feet on the table, and looked most undisturbed. When James stopped speaking, Rockefeller said calmly, "Now, James, you can knock my head off, but you might as well understand that you can't scare me." It was absolutely impossible to make Rockefeller bend his head or make him cower. After this little event, the relationship between the two men continued to slide downhill, but at least James never behaved that way again or anything near it in Rockefeller's presence. The bully had been put down by the seemingly robotic clerk.

Rockefeller argued with James about how to conduct business. He had also faced the same problem with his first partner, Maurice B. Clark. James would proudly say that he had tricked people and done dishonest things, and Rockefeller began to always keep an eye on the money that James spent. Like his brother, James saw Rockefeller's morality in the light of an unethical person. James nicknamed Rockefeller the "Sunday-school superintendent."

Rockefeller wanted to have around him people whom he could trust and who were honest. He wanted people who would not cause others to lose trust and confidence in them but rather stir trust in people who appealed to their services as well as the bankers.

Rockefeller believed that anyone who was not strong, unethical, and dishonest would live a life of failure. He said, "We were beginning to prosper, and I felt very uneasy at my name being linked up with these speculators." He basically did not want himself or his name to be associated with these rogues that were unfortunately his partners. The benefit of their having been his partners, however, was that perhaps they taught him how to choose people he could trust and bring into his business and those to keep as far away as possible from himself or his career.

Not long afterward the Clark brothers would come to share the same hatred that Rockefeller had for them for him. They would say bad things about Rockefeller and paint a negative picture of him simply because they disliked and hated him—a man who would become much richer and much more successful than they ever would be.

Rockefeller didn't like his first Clark partner not just because of who he was but also because of his perspective regarding the oil industry and how fast the industry should advance and grow.

When the Civil War raged on, the oil fields only stopped producing when the owners tried to protect their mines from the Confederates when General Robert Edward Lee attacked the state.

As the market for kerosene grew in overseas countries and was being exported, Andrew, Clark, and Company was able to make a tremendous amount of money.

Although all who were in the oil industry were greatly competitive, prices always fluctuated and never stabilized. In 1861, a barrel of oil would sometimes cost ten cents and at other times $10. In 1864, a barrel of oil would shift from $4 to $12.

Both Andrews and Rockefeller shared the same view: expand. They did not care for these small hiccups in the oil industry and wanted to grow their oil business. Clark, however, was not of that opinion. He wanted to be a little more cautious and was not so keen on involving himself too much in the oil industry.

What perhaps caused Rockefeller to leave his partners is that they were a majority party when it came to pushing his decisions aside. Andrews did not sympathize with Rockefeller but simply took advantage of the higher position of the three Clark brothers. Rockefeller once recounted an incident where Clark became upset with him because he had borrowed money to expand their oil business.

Rockefeller understood that unlike himself Clark was not one to take risks and would never do things that Rockefeller did. Clark was too scared. Rockefeller said, "Clark was an old grandmother and was scared to death because we owed money at the banks."

You could perhaps side with the Clarks because they were upset that their partner was using their money in an unstable venture that they thought should be done with caution. What the Clarks lacked, however, was foresight and confidence. Rockefeller understood that the oil industry would not wither away and thus did everything he could to dominate it. Perhaps if it hadn't been for Rockefeller the oil industry could've collapsed after a few years or decades, and that would have been the end of it. Perhaps the oil industry survived for as long as it did because Rockefeller believed it would be long-lasting, and his actions secured that fate, for his actions would carry the oil industry into the following centuries.

It 1865, Rockefeller thought it was time to finish the Clark brothers. He was just twenty-five years old at the time. His character prohibited him from continuing to be part of something that did not work well, and now he wanted to remove the hindrances in his life, which happened to be the Clark brothers.

For Rockefeller to fully immerse himself in the oil industry, he needed something to happen that would prove that the oil supply would not dry up. In January 1865, a place in Pithole Creek was sending up sulfuric gas from certain trenches in the land.

Some people were using a certain twig as a divining rod and then dug where the rod pointed. Several days later, oil came spewing from where they dug, and once again people were thrown into a frenzy. Pithole Creek used to be a calm and small area with just some houses made of logs, but just a few months later all kinds of people, from onlookers and oilmen to people representing businessmen, came to see the site. Very quickly, Pithole Creek's population soared to twelve thousand, and fifty hotels and even a theater were set up in the area.

One person who watched the frenzy at Pithole Creek was one Miss Ida Tarbell, who was just eight years old at the time and lived in Roseville, just ten miles from Pithole Creek. She would watch groups of people rush to Pithole. Her father opened a business that sold oil tanks, and he made money very quickly.

The frenzy at Pithole Creek ended after several years, for its oil wells had been burned and were exhausted. After the oil boom ended, people did what they could to survive with what was left of Pithole, which had turned into a bustling city. Tarbell's father purchased the Bonta House, a hotel in Pithole Creek, for just $600. It had cost $60,000 to build. He dismantled the hotel and used the pieces to build a home for his family in Titusville.

In 1874, after all the excitement came to an end, nine years after oil was struck in the area, the population had dwindled to just six people.

When you look back, Pithole's return to simplicity after the oil business in the area had collapsed seemed to indicate that the oil industry was not going to last very long. When the frenzy began, however, it seemed to prove that the oil industry would last a long time, and it also encouraged the break between the Clark brothers and Rockefeller. What miners and oil producers did not know was that there was still plenty of oil in the ground. The miners just didn't know how to get it out. In the past, they had relied on the internal pressure of the well to push the oil to the surface, but once that pressure equalized, the well stopped gushing. Today, we have all kinds of technologies to pump oil and exert pressure on the well as well as stimulation techniques, such as fracking.

What Rockefeller did to rid himself of the three Clark brothers was that he very slowly arranged everything and then quickly hit them with his plan before they had time to react.

Chapter 5 Strategic Mindset

"Next to doing the right thing, the most important thing is to let people know you are doing the right thing."

— John D. Rockefeller

When oil was struck in Pithole in January 1865, Rockefeller asked Clark to sign for another loan. Clark was incensed and didn't stay quiet. He said to Rockefeller, "We have been asking too many loans in order to extend this oil business." Rockefeller replied by saying, "We should borrow whenever we can safely extend the business by doing so."

To check Rockefeller, the three Clark brothers tried to intimidate him by saying they would break up the relationship between the partners by ending the partnership. To do this, all partners needed to agree, which would mean the end of the business. This was not the first or the last time that they tried to intimidate him by threatening dissolution, but Rockefeller knew their tricks and decided to use it for his benefit.

Rockefeller wanted to end his relationship with the Clark brothers and was done working in his current business of selling and buying on behalf of others. Rockefeller was able to get Andrews to join him in his venture to break from the Clark brothers.

He said to Andrews, "Sam, we are prospering. We have a future before us, a big future, but I don't like Jim Clark and his habits. He is an immoral man in more ways than one. He gambles in oil. I don't want this business to be associated with a gambler. Suppose I take them up the next time they threaten a dissolution. Suppose I succeed in buying them out. Will you come in with me?"

Andrews agreed to join Rockefeller since he, too, could plainly see that his fortunes would fare better with Rockefeller than with the crazy Clark brothers. Several weeks later the trigger for Rockefeller to enact his plan occurred. He had an argument with his first Clark partner, and

Clark said that he would break up the partnership of the produce firm. Clark said, "If that's the way you want to do business, we'd better dissolve and let you run your own affairs to suit yourself."

On February 1, 1865, Rockefeller made preparations for the final blow. He called his partners to his home and talked about ways they would expand their business in a manner that he knew the Clark brothers would absolutely dislike. Jim Clark tried to intimidate Rockefeller into backing off by saying, as before, "We'd better split up." Rockefeller then asked everyone to say whether or not they supported breaking up the partnership. They all did, but they were merely using it to threaten him, and when they left his house that night they thought nothing of it and thought they had gotten the better of him.

After the Clarks left his home, Rockefeller quickly rushed to the *Cleveland Leader* newspaper office and demanded an announcement to be printed in the papers that the partnership was breaking up. The newspaper ran the notice in the next morning's edition, and before even getting to the office, the brothers saw it.

When the Clark brothers saw this announcement, they were stunned. Rockefeller's first partner, Maurice B. Clark, asked Rockefeller, "Do you really mean it? You really want to break it up?" Rockefeller replied by saying, "I really want to break it up."

In the end, it was decided that the oil refinery part of Clark and Rockefeller would be auctioned off. It turned out that the bidders for the auction were Clark and Rockefeller themselves. Essentially, the buyout would mean that the company would either go to the Clark brothers or Rockefeller.

By this point, Rockefeller was a man who could handle the most troubling of situations with a clear mind and calm nerves. His character was also such that when the people around him became more upset he became even more poised.

When the Clark brothers went to the auction, they had a lawyer with them, who was the auctioneer himself. Rockefeller, however, did not bring a lawyer of his own. He thought he could handle it himself.

The bidding began at $500. It then increased to several thousand dollars. Then it reached $50,000, $60,000, and $70,000. By this point, Rockefeller was afraid that he would not be able to make the purchase. Then the Clarks put up $72,000, and Rockefeller quickly bid $72,500. Clark let go at that point, and Rockefeller asked, "Shall I give you a check for it now?" Clark demurred and said that Rockefeller could pay when he was ready. It was a gentlemanly gesture, and it came with a shock in his voice, as he had no idea that Rockefeller had amassed that much money to make the purchase.

It turned out that Rockefeller's strategy of being prudent and bankable worked in his favor. When the time came, he had lined up a line of credit from the banks that supported his takeover of the company. It was with their backing that he had the strength and tenacity to bid the price up to that level.

The price of $72,500 in 1865 would be about $1.2 million today. Although the price was expensive for the time, it was an important purchase. Rockefeller was just twenty-five years old and now owner of the largest oil refinery in Cleveland, which was refining five hundred barrels of oil every day. Approximately two weeks after the Clarks met with Rockefeller in his home, the *Cleveland Leader* announced that Rockefeller had purchased the firm of Andrews, Clark and Company. It went on to say that Rockefeller had purchased all the materials of the company, and that they would continue their work under the firm of Rockefeller and Andrews.

Chapter 6 Family

"I do not think that there is any other quality so essential to success of any kind as the quality of perseverance. It overcomes almost everything, even nature."

— John D. Rockefeller

The year before the breakup between the Clarks and Rockefeller, Rockefeller married his wife, Laura Celestia Spelman, who was also known as Cettie. The two had met in high school, and Rockefeller was also acquainted with Laura's sister. Her father was Harvey Buel Spelman. He had been a businessman, whose businesses sometimes fell flat, leaving the family in a state of poverty. The Spelman family was always insecure by not knowing when the next round of money was coming.

After moving to Cleveland, the family was better off, and Harvey's business did well.

Unfortunately, it all later collapsed, and Harvey and Laura's mother left Cleveland. To help, Laura and her sister stayed behind in Cleveland and worked as schoolteachers.

Laura strongly supported not drinking and was a devout Baptist. During her marriage with Rockefeller, she would be the strict and stern one, while Rockefeller was the fun one, but they were a match made in heaven.

The entire Spelman family strongly supported the abolition of slavery and did not just sit by the sidelines and wait for that time to come. The Spelman home was a place along the Underground Railroad where slaves were able to flee from the slave drivers and owners of the South to the free land of the North.

Laura's mother would cook food for the slaves making their way along the Underground Railroad, and the entire family devoted themselves to helping them.

Rockefeller's background was quite different from Laura's. At the time of the marriage, her family was rather well-to-do, and she was living a comfortable life but did not indulge in it. Rockefeller, on the other hand, had a rather rough background and was not very wealthy. Still, the two would make it work.

Before their marriage, Rockefeller would go to her home, and they would go over his ledgers, something they both loved. As time went by, Laura's relationship with Rockefeller became less of a loving one and more of a friendship. When Rockefeller became more wealthy, however, he would try ever harder to win her.

In the end, they were married September 8, 1864, in Cleveland. They would have five children: four daughters and one son: Alice, Edith, Elizabeth, Alta, and John. Alice Rockefeller died just after her first birthday. Rockefeller was very close to his wife and took her very seriously. As he said, "Her judgment was always better than mine. Without her keen advice, I would be a poor man."

All of their children were raised to be very pious, devout, and clean people. They were virtually locked up in the family home and shielded from the outside world and the immense wealth of the

Rockefeller family. They were raised as if they were poor. Rockefeller Jr. wore his sisters' hand-me-down dresses and skirts until he was eight years old! All of the children shared their toys among themselves.

When Laura was once speaking to a neighbor, she said she was so glad that her son had told her what he wanted for Christmas because, according to her, they could now say "No" to him.

The Rockefeller children were raised to not indulge in money, and one of the quotes from the Bible that Rockefeller Jr. committed to memory was "It is easier for a camel to go through the eye of a needle than for a rich man to enter the kingdom of God." When John Jr. was ten years old, he was made to swear that he would never smoke or drink. Unfortunately, he would break part of that oath by smoking a packet of cigarettes.

Although the Rockefeller home was grand and nicely built, the interior was bare of any luxuries, and everyone lived simply.

Laura had a certain practice with the children. Every Sunday all of them would sit down and confess what wrongs they had committed that week and would prepare themselves to do better the coming week. The entire Rockefeller family was very pious and enlightened. Laura and Rockefeller were already that way, and their children were being molded to become that way.

Between the two parents, Rockefeller was by far the much more entertaining one. While Laura would discipline the children, Rockefeller would play with them. He would have bicycle chases with them in the large land area of their family home, and he would teach them how to ice-skate. Whenever Rockefeller won a bicycle race, he would act like a young child and cry in joy. He naturally loved children and greatly loved his own.

Chapter 7 Standard Oil

"I always tried to turn every disaster into an opportunity."

— **John D. Rockefeller**

Five years after the breakup between Rockefeller and the Clarks, Rockefeller established Standard Oil of Ohio. Other cofounders included Rockefeller's brother, William Rockefeller Jr., Henry Huttleston Rogers, and Henry Flagler.

With the founding of Standard Oil of Ohio behind him and the refineries of Rockefeller and Andrews absorbed into Standard Oil of Ohio (Sohio), Rockefeller set out to take control of the other twenty-six oil refineries in Cleveland. His main goal was to be the sole oil refiner in the world, but his first goal was Ohio. Within two months from the time he began acquiring control of the other oil refineries, he had taken over twenty-two of them.

He took control of the oil refineries either through a friendly approach or coercion. He would at first talk cordially with the owners of the refineries and try to get them to sell their company to him on their own volition. If that didn't work, he would proceed to force them to sell their company to him. Rockefeller did not like forcing people to do something and preferred getting them to do it themselves, but he was not going to let that get in the way of his success and did what was needed to get the job done.

To cut costs and be in a more advantageous position, he made a deal with the railroad companies known as the South Improvement Company. He would give the railroads more business by giving them his oil to transport, and in return they would charge him lower prices for their services. Meanwhile, they would continue to charge other customers regular rates, which were quite expensive.

Rockefeller was thus able to achieve a superior position in transporting his oil at lower cost and beat out his competitors. Standard Oil operated on a global scale. It was not just confined to the United States, and any competing oil refinery, if not careful, would become prey of the Standard Oil Trust (which was yet to come).

Global Oil

To deepen this facet of Standard Oil, it has to be seen in the context of the global oil industry. Sir Marcus Samuel was a man who worked in the business of buying seashells from the Middle East and selling them to those who were using them as decorations. He and his brother, Sam, also worked in the business of sending goods to Japan and buying from them such things as silk, rice, and other Eastern commodities. Samuel's interest in the oil business sparked when he traveled to Japan.

At this time, the French banking family the Rothschilds had put their money into building railroads and passages through which oil could be transported. Transporting oil was still difficult to do, and shipping was inefficient, as the barrels took up too much space. Finally,

Marcus and his brother had a large number of ships transport the oil in barrels.

Instead, however, of loading cargo ships with barrels, which themselves took up space and weight, they decided to make tankers. Their first tanker, which needed to be approved by the Suez Canal Company to be able to pass through its canal from the Mediterranean to the Red Sea, was approved. The oil tanker *Murex* transported a large quantity of oil to Thailand, and Marcus was successful in changing the way oil was transported. He was able to reduce transportation costs of oil for purchasers.

In 1897, five years after the success of the *Murex*, the Samuel brothers renamed their company The "Shell" Transport and Trading Company Limited. It was originally called The Tank Syndicate.

In the East Indies, it was the Royal Dutch Petroleum Company, which had been established in 1890 by King William III of the Netherlands. Because its competitor The "Shell" Transport and Trading Company was able to transport oil at a lower cost, the Royal Dutch

Petroleum Company began to build oil tankers for themselves. To be strong enough to compete against the Standard Oil Trust of John D. Rockefeller, in 1903 the Royal Dutch Petroleum Company and The Shell Transport and Trading Company joined to form the Asiatic Petroleum Company.

The following year the first form of what is today the symbol of Shell, the pecten, became the company's logo. Previously, the logo was the shell of a mussel. In 1907, the Asiatic Petroleum Company would become Royal Dutch Shell, also known as the Shell Oil Company.

Out of mere fear of Standard Oil, this was how Royal Dutch Shell came into existence. Shell is now the fifth largest oil company in the world, just behind ExxonMobil, a company that resulted from the breakup of Standard Oil.

The fact that Shell was created on the basis of fear of Standard Oil shows that Rockefeller's power was more than just domination over the industry. It shows that competitors feared destruction from the oil titan. Rockefeller's Standard Oil Trust was more than just an extremely large oil refining company. It was a formidable competitor.

Standard Oil was built upon clever tactics and strategies. Rockefeller may have bribed a few politicians to his benefit, but you can't consider that to have been wrong on his part. All successful businessmen cannot be by-the-book and neat and tidy. They need to do whatever is necessary to get what they want done.

When Rockefeller had to pay off politicians, he viewed paying them as if they were in a higher position than he was rather than considering them as puny, corrupt politicians that he could control.

Chapter 8 Monopolies, Electricity, and Alcohol

"Good leadership consists of showing average people how to do the work of superior people."

— **John D. Rockefeller**

In 1879, Thomas Alva Edison perfected the light bulb, and shortly afterward J.P. Morgan financed Edison and worked with him to make electricity widespread and the dominant fuel for lights in America. This was a serious problem for Rockefeller, for Standard Oil was at the time supplying kerosene to people, and it was being used as an illuminant. If electricity replaced kerosene, Rockefeller was going to lose a large market for his product.

So, he set out to stop the advance of electricity by saying bad things about it and reporting these things to the press, hoping that the American people would become afraid of electricity and not use it.

Unfortunately for Rockefeller, his attempts to stop the advance of electricity did not work, and it came to be the dominant power source in the United States, causing Rockefeller to lose his customers who were buying kerosene for their lights.

Something else would soon open up for Rockefeller, however, which was the automobile industry. The first car of modern times was invented by German inventor Karl Benz in 1885. The cars ran on gasoline, something that Standard Oil was happy to supply.

The problem, though, was that electric cars were also being used in the United States. The first electric car had been created in 1884 and posed a threat to such people as Rockefeller. Electric streetcars bused people from one part of a city to another part and powered personal vehicles.

In the end, General Motors, one of the largest automobile companies in the world, would begin to tear down the streetcars and use that material to build their buses, which ran on gasoline whose supplier was Standard Oil.

It is difficult to believe that Standard Oil ended up being the supplier of gasoline for the company that took down the electric streetcars, benefiting Rockefeller's empire just by coincidence. Perhaps he had a hand in the monopolization of the transportation business by General Motors (GM).

The main cause of the downfall of the electric car industry was that an oil derrick began gushing out one hundred thousand barrels of oil a day, dramatically reducing the price of oil, kerosene, and gasoline. Electric cars were extremely expensive, and now that gasoline was a much cheaper alternative, the American people favored that over electric cars. This led to the decline in popularity of the electric car and the rise of vehicles powered by gasoline.

Thus, Standard Oil was rid of the electric car industry and could continue to supply gasoline to customers. Rockefeller was once again at the top, able to supply his oil to the country. Although he had lost the battle against electricity as an illuminant, he managed to succeed in supplying the fledgling automobile industry with a power source: gasoline.

As for alcohol, at one time the automobile industry used alcohol as a fuel source. Those who opposed titans and such large corporations as Standard Oil from dominating an industry supported the use of alcohol as a fuel.

Again, there was a threat to Rockefeller's oil empire. If alcohol became the dominant fuel for cars, Rockefeller would lose his market, as he had lost his market when electricity became the dominant illuminant.

The problem at the time was that Americans drank a lot of alcohol. They drank much more than the average American does today. The average teenager at least fifteen years old was drinking seven gallons of alcohol per year, and people began protesting against it. Howard Hyde Russell founded the Anti-Saloon League, or ASL, to which Rockefeller donated a lot of money.

The intoxicating effects of alcohol and the high drinking rate of the American people led to

Prohibition, which lasted from 1920 to 1933. Those that were selling alcohol as a fuel for cars had to mix petroleum with their alcohol so that it would be poisonous, preventing the purchaser from consuming it. It thus became very expensive to use alcohol as a fuel, and the industry declined, allowing Rockefeller to continue supplying the American public with gasoline for their automobiles.

Rockefeller had capitalized on the American people's opposition to alcohol. He had used that to his benefit so stop alcohol from being used as a fuel source and bring gasoline, which was largely supplied by Standard Oil, back to the market.

Perhaps Rockefeller was behind the fall of electric cars in the nineteenth century and also partially behind the beginning of Prohibition, thus allowing him to eliminate two industries— the electric car and alcohol as fuel. Rockefeller's tactics to place his company at the head of the game was what made it a success, but it was also what made him and his company greatly despised by the American people.

Rockefeller's power was so great that he was able to influence the course of American history. He did what was needed to keep his company at the top and maintain the success of his multinational empire, which, if it hadn't been broken up, would be the largest oil company in the world today.

Chapter 9 Heir to the Throne

"I would rather earn 1% off a 100 people's efforts than 100% of my own efforts."

— **John D. Rockefeller**

John D. Rockefeller Jr. was quite different from his father. He was a much more easygoing person and danced, against his mother's liking, but was also a much more timid and unsure person.

John Jr. could've gone to Yale University but chose to go to Brown University. After graduation, he worked at Standard Oil. There, he was given all the necessities of working in the company but was not told his particular duties. Rockefeller Sr. had retired from Standard Oil in 1897, and John Jr. was responsible for carrying on the business. It was much too stressful for him, though, and he very quickly quit working at

Standard Oil and devoted himself to philanthropy and bettering the family name.

At a dance that John Jr. attended, he met Abigail Greene Aldrich, the daughter of Senator Nelson Wilmarth Aldrich of Rhode Island. Senator Aldrich was the man whose actions led to the formation of the Federal Reserve System. Abigail, or Abby as she was also known, would go on to found the Museum of Modern Art.

On October 9, 1901, the couple were married in Aldrich Mansion at Warwick Neck on Rhode Island. Standard Oil directors attended the ceremony as did directors of several other companies.

Their marriage was seen as a fusion of money and politics—an alliance between the wealthy Rockefellers and the political Aldrich family.

Together, they had six children: Abigail, also known as Abby, John D. Rockefeller III, Nelson, Laurance, Winthrop, and David. Nelson Rockefeller was later vice president of the United States under President Gerald Ford. He ran for president four times and would have won had he not married a woman who was already a mother. His campaign was going well until his marriage, and from then on people started to dislike him.

David Rockefeller was later CEO, chairman, and president of Chase National Bank.

David's grandfather, John D. Rockefeller Sr., had been the largest shareholder of Chase Bank.

Rockefeller had wished to live until he was 100 years old. He didn't, as he died when he was 97, but his grandson, David Rockefeller, lived until he was 101, being born in 1915 and passing in 2017 before his 102nd birthday.

After having left Standard Oil in 1910, John Jr. began repairing the family name, for it had been tarnished by muckraking reporters, such as Ida Tarbell, a reporter for *McClure's* Magazine.

His philanthropy included preserving areas, rebuilding sites, and dedicating lands to the public. Everything he did was to make the Rockefeller name shine and change the way it was being seen by the American public.

When everything was proceeding satisfactorily, something extremely disastrous occurred. Workers at the Colorado Fuel and Iron Company, which was controlled by Rockefeller Sr., went on strike. They demanded higher salaries and safer working conditions.

The CFI Company kicked the workers out of their homes since they were provided by the company, and the workers and their families were forced to camp out in tents. The National Guard was called to take care of the situation, as the Ludlow Massacre took place on April 20, 1914, when the workers were fired on by machine guns, but many workers were able to escape the carnage, for a train came through that day, blocking the National Guard of Colorado and the guards of CFI from the workers.

The brakeman of the train said he saw one of the men walking in the workers camp and setting it on fire. People hid in underground compartments. When everything was over, two women and eleven children were found inside one of them. Twenty-four people died that day.

The Ludlow Massacre, as it is known, was attributed to the Rockefellers.

John Jr. tried his best to solve the situation. He travelled to Ludlow to see the people. He spent time with them—eating, dancing, and doing his best to make everything good again. In the end, everything turned out well, and John Sr. gave John Jr. a large number of shares of the Colorado Fuel and Iron Company.

A great many Americans did not like the Rockefellers, and the family received ominous threats. John Sr. was pushed to the point that he began keeping a loaded revolver next to him when he slept. Threats of kidnapping and even bomb threats were also made.

These threats were particularly startling for John Jr. because his mother, who was now in poor health, was living in the family home of Kykuit in Sleepy Hollow, New York.

One time a bomb that was believed meant to arrive at the Rockefeller home exploded before it got there, and four people were killed.

To consider how the Rockefeller name was tarnished and why so many people disliked and despised the Rockefeller family, the reporter Ida Tarbell must be mentioned.

Chapter 10 The Three Titans

"I have ways of making money that you know nothing of."

— **John D. Rockefeller**

In 1896, William Jennings Bryan was running for president. He opposed big business and large corporations, such as Standard Oil, Carnegie Steel, and J.P. Morgan and Company. Bryan was the ultimate enemy of the titans of America. If he became president, all of them, including John D. Rockefeller, Andrew Carnegie, and J.P. Morgan, and their companies, would be severely threatened by his policies.

To avert disaster, they joined forces to defeat Bryan and install a president in the White House whom they favored. They wanted Republican William McKinley. Unlike Bryan, McKinley supported large corporations and big businesses and would be the perfect president for them.

Bryan appealed to the working class, which felt they had had enough of the wealthy men of America who had millions of dollars while they were earning less than a dollar a day. Workers for Carnegie and Rockefeller worked in extremely intolerable conditions in front of extremely hot furnaces and in oil refineries. They wanted better working conditions. These were the Populists, and William Jennings Bryan appealed to them in the presidential election.

If Bryan became president, everything that Andrew Carnegie, John D. Rockefeller, and J.P. Morgan had spent their lives building would be seriously threatened. They needed William McKinley in the White House, so each of them donated more than $200,000 to his campaign. Even $250,000 back then would be $7,477,172.62 today. If they donated $750,000, that would be about $22 million today.

In the end, William McKinley won the 1896 election and became president of the United States. They were safe—for now.

After having succeeded in getting McKinley elected president, the alliance between Morgan,

Carnegie, and Rockefeller was no longer necessary. Rockefeller was the first to break from the group. He wanted to find a way to hurt Andrew Carnegie and looked into the steel industry, something Rockefeller actually did not have any interest in at all. He began mining at a certain iron ore mine that Carnegie had brushed off as unimportant. Rockefeller then began selling the iron ore to Carnegie's competitors and was making a nice profit. Carnegie's competitors were also able to have more business and were making more steel.

Rockefeller wasn't the only one causing trouble for Carnegie. Rockefeller had been selling the components of steel to rival steel manufacturers, who believed that perhaps they could sell their steel for slightly cheaper prices than Carnegie did and would get more customers.

The effects on Carnegie Steel were drastic. Within just a few months, the profits of the company reduced dramatically, and Andrew Carnegie had to do something. The worst was still to come. Rockefeller was planning to build a steel mill to hurt his rival even more. Carnegie could not let him do that. If Rockefeller entered the steel industry on a full-fledged scale, Carnegie's steel empire would be under invasion.

Carnegie set out to try to use fear to stop Rockefeller from entering the steel industry, but that wasn't going to work. The two began talks, which lasted for months, and nothing happened. Finally, Carnegie understood that he had to give in and proposed to buy the iron ore mine from Rockefeller, and Rockefeller was to stop building his steel mill. In the end, Rockefeller was able to get Carnegie to pay him a large sum of money to sell something to him that Rockefeller didn't much care for and not build the steel plant that Rockefeller also did not have any interest in.

Rockefeller displayed both a keen intelligence and ruthlessness in this act of business, but you cannot say that he was cruel. That is how proper business is done and how one becomes successful.

This incident shows that Rockefeller was someone who did not care for being delicate and tidy. He only cared about success and doing what he had to do to win. He did not care for niceties and focused on the goal. After realizing what he wanted to do, he got it done in whatever way he had to regardless of how it was seen by the masses.

One thing they had in common was that they would send each other Christmas gifts, although these gifts were more out of spite than being sincere. Rockefeller once sent Carnegie a brown vest made of paper. It was meant to highlight Carnegie's poor background as a migrant from a foreign country. Carnegie, knowing that Rockefeller was a staunch nondrinker, sent him a bottle of liquor.

As they aged and their thoughts turned to their own mortality, the race became more about legacy than pranks. The two began a new race. This time the race was to see how much they could give to charity.

Chapter 11 Ida Tarbell

"After it is all over, the religion of man is his most important possession."

— John D. Rockefeller

Muckraking journalist Ida Minerva Tarbell wrote a nineteen-part exposé of Standard Oil and John D. Rockefeller. In her scathing series, she harshly criticized Rockefeller and Standard Oil for being cruel and ruthless. More than just chasing after a good story and wanting to reveal the "truth" of Standard Oil and Rockefeller, she actually had a personal score to settle with both.

Tarbell's father had been in the oil industry at the beginning along with her brother. They were both destroyed because of Standard Oil, and Tarbell built up personal animosity and hatred for John D. Rockefeller and his oil empire.

She was not the only one who was criticizing and rebuking Standard Oil. The press and many people did not like the company or him.

Rockefeller was characterized as a greedy monster who hoarded all his money and hurt others to make money. He was portrayed as a ruthless serpent—an evil force plaguing the American people and the industry.

Her series about Standard Oil was deeply hurtful to the entire Rockefeller family. She harshly criticized the company and Rockefeller. She made it appear that Standard Oil had been built upon deceit, cruelty, ruthlessness, and evil. She made John D. Rockefeller the personification of evil in people's minds, and it is very probable that she really believed it too.

The last two parts of her Standard Oil series were centered more on Rockefeller himself. She described Rockefeller as extremely ugly and looked like a leper. She had actually seen him once. He was walking, and according to her, he was watching everyone, looking for those who may be his adversaries.

At one point, the family employed members of the Pinkerton Detectives to protect their home. These were mercenary fighters willing to fight if the price suited them.

John Jr. devoted his life to repairing the family name, trying to undo the damage that had been caused by Ida Tarbell and all those who rebuked Standard Oil and his father.

Her actions led to passage of the Sherman Antitrust Act in 1890, legislation that would cause trouble for not just Rockefeller but also for many more businessmen, including J.P. Morgan, whose company would be broken up.

Before the breakup of Standard Oil, investigations had been opened into the company, and Rockefeller was called to appear in court. He did not want to appear, though, and ran.

He kept running and running, and no one knew for sure where he had gone. Finally, what made him return was the birth of his grandchild. He did not want to be an absent grandfather and decided to return and appear in court.

He fought the court for some time until the Supreme Court ruled that the Standard Oil Trust was to be dissolved. Rockefeller was accused of creating a monopoly, and the takeover of the oil industry in Cleveland was dubbed the Cleveland Massacre. In the end, despite Rockefeller's best attempts, Standard Oil was dissolved in 1911.

The company was broken down into thirty-four other companies, including Esso, Sohio, Calso, Kyso, Chevron, Amoco, and Mobil.

Calso, which was Standard Oil of California, later took over Standard Oil of Kentucky, or Kyso. Later on, it took control of Texaco and became ChevronTexaco. In 2005, it took over UNOCAL and is known today as Chevron or Chevron Corporation.

Standard Oil of New York joined with MobilGas in 1931 and was later rechristened Mobil in 1963.

Esso, Standard Oil of New Jersey, joined with Humble Gas in 1959 and was rechristened Exxon in 1973. In 1999, Mobil and Exxon joined to form ExxonMobil, the fourth largest oil company in the world.

Service, or Standard Oil of Indiana, became Amoco in 1925 and in 1998 was taken up by the British Petroleum Company, or BP. Standard Oil of Ohio, or Sohio, was also taken up by BP in 1987. Finally, the Ohio Oil Company became Marathon in 1930 and Marathon Petroleum in 2011.

The breakup of Standard Oil made Rockefeller even richer. He was a major shareholder in all the companies, and a certain percentage of their profits went to him. When the automobile industry progressed with the production of the Model T, where almost everyone had a car, the successors of Standard Oil were providing the fuel, and large amounts of cash kept coming in.

Before and after the Standard Oil breakup in 1911, Rockefeller worked hard to restore his image. He had been portrayed as this savage, brutal, cruel, and ruthless monster who had monopolized the oil industry. His company was depicted in cartoons as an octopus strangling the world. He had dominated the oil refining industry in such a cunning and do-whatever-you-have-to way that people despised both him and his company.

So, he set out to repair his image. He began giving dimes to people in the street. He filmed videos of himself and did his best to seem like a very nice person. One video shows him getting in a plane that goes down the runway but doesn't take off. It was meant to look like John D. Rockefeller's first time in an airplane. After the stunt, the video filmed Rockefeller giving a dime to each of the two people who "took him up" in the plane. Someone out of view of the camera had suggested that he give dimes to them.

All in all, Rockefeller gave about thirty thousand dimes to people. Slowly, he began to be regarded as a nice old man rather than a greedy monster.

John Jr. established many parks, restored many areas, and was more of a people person than his father. He built Rockefeller Center, a towering office building in New York City. He dedicated the better part of his entire life, and by the time he passed in his eighties, he had accomplished his goal. The Rockefeller name had been repaired, and the damage done by such journalists as Ida Tarbell was over. By the time John Jr. passed away, the Rockefeller name was no longer a subject of hate and anger but one of much more cordial essences.

Chapter 12 Pipelines, Railroads, and Corruption

"I know of nothing more despicable and pathetic than a man who devotes all the hours of the waking day to the making of money for money's sake."

— **John D. Rockefeller**

Rockefeller's business was not just limited to refineries. He had also dealt in the storage business and pipelines. He had oil tanks that producers could use to store their crude oil, and the pipelines were used to transport oil.

In the 1870s, a certain geologist predicted that the oil reserves in the world would run dry very quickly, causing fear in the hearts of those who worked in the oil industry and who had thought the oil industry would skyrocket. This prediction was proven wrong, however, when yet more oil was struck in Bradford, Pennsylvania. Fortune seekers and young men raced to capitalize on the discovery. So much was being produced that the price for a single barrel of oil dropped to seventy cents a barrel. It used to be $4 a barrel!

As more and more oil wells were established in Bradford, Rockefeller connected them to his vast network of pipelines to continue his hold on the pipeline business. His storage tanks began to fill to full capacity until he could no longer store the oil that was being drilled.

In response to the problem, Standard Oil instituted the policy of immediately shipping the oil that producers drilled. Standard Oil's storage space was overfull, and producers were not allowed to store their oil. They had to send it immediately to refineries. Rockefeller wanted this oil to go to the refineries of Standard Oil. He was buying the oil from the producers at a price less than the market value by 20 percent and would not pay them immediately. The producers were naturally upset. Not only were they coerced into shipping their oil immediately, but they were also selling it for very low prices and not being paid at the time.

Rockefeller had taken advantage of the storage crisis and was able to benefit from it. He couldn't store the oil for lack of space, so he took the oil and shipped it to his refineries.

People did not like his behavior though. They dressed in white gowns from head to foot and protested in the streets against Standard Oil. They vandalized the buildings of Standard Oil and drew the signature pirate symbol of a skull and crossbones on the walls of the buildings.

To scare those who were drilling for oil, William McCandless was chosen to investigate and closely analyze the oil industry. He went after Standard Oil, but its pipeline executives simply ignored him. Surprisingly, in October 1878, McCandless submitted a report that vindicated Standard Oil. People believed that he might have been bribed by Rockefeller, which could be true. Rockefeller was capable and completely willing to give money under the table if necessary.

An effigy of McCandless was made and hung in Bradford. In the pocket of the dummy was a large check signed by John D. Rockefeller for $20,000.

After this issue, the Pennsylvania Railroad Company would also cause trouble for Rockefeller. Thomas Alexander Scott wanted to ease the monopoly that Standard Oil enjoyed over oil transportation. The PRR Co. had railroads near Bradford, and Scott was plotting to loosen the Standard Oil monopoly.

Colonel Jacob Potts, a man who wanted to be John D. Rockefeller's biggest competitor, did what he could to achieve that goal. He was deeply religious and treated the oil industry as he did his religion. When Potts crossed the line, Rockefeller wanted to meet with Thomas Scott and A.J. Cassatt. Both men were with the Pennsylvania Railroad Company.

Scott was essentially threatening the Standard Oil monopoly, and Rockefeller fought back. He ceased all production in his refineries in Pittsburgh and ramped up production in his Cleveland refineries. Instead of using the Pennsylvania Railroad Company to transport his oil, Rockefeller used the New York Central and the Erie Railroad. To transport the oil, cofounder of Standard Oil Henry Flagler made a deal with William Vanderbilt, son of Cornelius Vanderbilt, to build six hundred oil tank cars.

The Pennsylvania Railroad Company had to keep reducing rates to remain stable, as Rockefeller was skillfully fighting back against it and Scott.

After some time, the company could not continue the fight, and Scott wanted to make a truce with Rockefeller, but Potts wanted to prolong the duel. Not wanting to damage the Pennsylvania Railroad Company any further, Scott went behind Potts' back and tried to make a deal with Rockefeller to smooth things over and end the feud. Rockefeller responded kindly to make peace with him.

Scott offered Rockefeller all the assets of the Empire Transportation Company through which he had tried to sabotage Standard Oil. These included boats, barges, and all sorts of transportation equipment. Rockefeller spent half a day running around trying to get money. Standard Oil didn't have enough cash to buy everything Scott was offering them.

Despite the problems, Rockefeller was very happy with what he achieved.

After that issue with the Pennsylvania Railroad Company, Rockefeller would face the Tidewater Pipe Company, a company cofounded by Byron Benson, which would set to work building six-inch wide pipelines from Coryville to Williamsport, both in Pennsylvania, for the purpose of transporting oil and breaking the Standard Oil monopoly. Rockefeller could not let this happen, for it would threaten his domination over the pipeline business.

The Tidewater Pipe Company's pipeline from Coryville to Williamsport was 110 miles long. During its construction, Rockefeller's right-hand man would carry out his dirty work to try and prevent the construction of the Coryville-Williamsport pipeline.

Before the pipeline was built, Rockefeller ordered that it be stopped. Despite his best efforts, however, they were unsuccessful.

After the building began, Rockefeller's people worked hard to stop it. They bribed legislators and used unscrupulous methods to try and stop construction. They purchased stretches of land and got railroads to not allow the Tidewater Pipe Company to build pipelines under their land.

Rockefeller even purchased a vast expanse of land hoping to stop construction of the pipeline, but it didn't work. The builders simply built around the bought-up land. Despite Rockefeller's best attempts, construction of the Coryville-Williamsport pipeline was completed in less than ninety days.

Oil was pumped from Coryville, and people watched earnestly as the oil slowly made its way to Williamsport, making the Tidewater Pipe Company successful in having bypassed the Standard Oil Trust. The Tidewater Pipe Company had defeated Standard Oil and succeeded in building a pipeline that transported oil that did not belong to John D. Rockefeller or Standard Oil Trust.

Because of Rockefeller's associates' tactics and strategies to try to defeat the Tidewater Pipe Company, the American government and people wanted them behind bars. Many of the people who worked for Standard Oil were called to testify before court. Rockefeller, however, was not needed to appear in court.

He was very worried about the case, and for the next thirty years of his life, starting in the 1880s, he would keep as far away from the law as he could. During one summer, he spent his time at Forest Hill, where he could be safe.

After suffering from a long period of worry and distress, Standard Oil finally pledged that it would return to the norms of business. It would buy products at market price and play fairly. It was all a facade, though, as was later revealed.

Chapter 13 Philanthropy

"Giving should be entered into in just the same
way as investing. Giving is investing."

— John D. Rockefeller

During the 1880s, people were constantly pestering Rockefeller for money. He enjoyed peace, solitude, and being nice and calm. Large throngs of money-hungry people following him robbed him of those things he cherished.

Rockefeller said that they would be there during and after dinner when all he would've liked to do was to chit-chat with his family until it was time to go to bed. They would constantly be badgering him for money, and he really couldn't stand it. They would eat with him, walk to his office that was at 26 Broadway with him, walk back with him to his home, and would basically be real pests.

Rockefeller wanted to fix this problem. He understood that you can't really do philanthropic work unless you help solve a problem. Rockefeller's view of philanthropy was that he only cared about solving the main problem, not doing small, menial things that helped that individual person for a short time but not in the long term. Rockefeller believed in doing philanthropic work for the sake of helping the masses.

He wanted to use his money intelligently, and he was going to do it through charity. He was going to use his money to help people in a substantial way. Perhaps his most noteworthy philanthropic work was establishing the University of Chicago in 1890.

In the late 1880s, Baptist minister Augustus H. Strong, an associate of Rockefeller's, wanted to build a university for Baptists in New York City of which he would be master. He kept pestering Rockefeller to fund his idea, but Rockefeller wasn't very enthusiastic about it. Strong continued to talk to him until Rockefeller banned discussion of the subject.

The relationship between Rockefeller and Strong became more personal as the relationship between the Rockefeller family and that of the Strongs became closer. Whenever Strong came to Cleveland, he and his family were one of the few people who rarely ever came to the Rockefeller home in Forest Hill. Strong's son, Charles, was friends with the Rockefeller children, but in the beginning Rockefeller and Laura were afraid that Charles would damage their religious core. The Rockefeller children and Charles got along perfectly well, though, and their relationship was fine. In the beginning, Charles liked Alta, but later he grew to like Elizabeth, or Bessie, as she was also known. Later on, Bessie and Charles would become husband and wife.

Bessie later went to Vassar, a girls school that had been chosen for her since the elder Strong was a trustee on the school's board of trustees. She had eye problems and thus had trouble reading, so it was arranged that she didn't have to take the entrance exam and that she could share a room with someone who would read the books to her. It was at Vassar that Rockefeller met the first president of the University of Chicago, William Rainey Harper.

Harper was a prodigy when he was at Muskingum College at the age of ten. He graduated when he was fourteen and received his PhD when he was just eighteen years old. Harper was an ardent Baptist whom Rockefeller grew to like. When Rockefeller came to Vassar to see his daughter on the weekends, he would always dine with Harper. They developed a very close relationship and would often cycle together.

Harper taught at Yale University but came to Vassar to teach Bible classes on Sundays.

Rockefeller and Harper talked about building a school for Baptists in a well-to-do urban center, but Harper made the mistake of pressuring Rockefeller. Another person who had done that before was Augustus H. Strong. He had made the fatal mistake of pressuring and pestering Rockefeller for his university. Rockefeller did not like being pressured. If you wanted something from him, you needed to calmly and coolly ask him for it. If you pressured him and pestered him, he'd dislike you at once and wouldn't consider your wishes. Harper had complied with Rockefeller's wishes to not talk about the issue of building a university, but when he brought it up again, he headed down a path that ruined his dreams, and Rockefeller dismissed the idea.

Not wanting to exclude Strong due to their family relations, Rockefeller invited Strong to travel with him to Europe. Strong accepted his invitation, seeing that it was a good way to press his idea on Rockefeller.

The relationship between Charles Strong and Elizabeth Rockefeller became very deep indeed, but a disaster, or actually an awakening, came over Charles, ripping him away from the Baptist Church. His time at Harvard University and his outside influences had led him to leave the Baptist Church, and he realized that none of it was real. This revelation was a great disappointment to his father.

Augustus had trained Charles to live a Baptist life of piety. Now, all his dreams, hopes, and

157

expectations for his son were shattered, but they decided not to speak about it to the Rockefellers.

So, Charles proceeded with his relationship with Bessie, and Augustus continued to pressure Rockefeller to fund his university. In the end, the couple married on March 22, 1889.

William Harper and Baptist priest Frederick Taylor Gates would also convince Rockefeller to build the University of Chicago.

Harper had failed, initially, in trying to convince Rockefeller, but Gates, being a man who knew how to talk to people and convince them without upsetting them, was able to get Rockefeller on board with building the university.

Gates was always there to advise Rockefeller on his philanthropic work and worked closely with him in building of the University of Chicago.

For Rockefeller to build a university really did seem quite strange. He himself had never gone to a university, and he never suggested others to go to college either. He still agreed to build the university, however, thanks to Harper and Gates. He had been told that the only Baptist schools were in backwater areas. In the minds of these Baptists who were trying to establish the university, a Baptist educational institute was needed in an urban center.

Rockefeller kept delaying giving money for the university, but eventually proposed $400,000. Gates said it wasn't enough, and when Rockefeller offered $500,000, Gates said it still wasn't enough. Finally, $600,000 was accepted, and the university was supposed to raise another $400,000.

Unfortunately, William Harper, who later became the first president of the University of Chicago, was not able to raise the necessary funds. In fact, he spent too much money in other ventures. He wanted to upgrade from college level to university standards in a flash. Rockefeller favored a more gradual approach, one where the school started off as a college and slowly evolved to become a university.

The University of Chicago was established in 1890, and William Rainer Harper was its first president, beginning in 1890 and ending in 1906 upon his passing. When it first began, the university had 750 students, of which a portion were women, another extremely small number were Jewish, and some blacks were also in the group.

Harper expanded the university and persuaded other professors to come and teach there. So, the university had a moderate number of students in the beginning as well as high-quality teachers.

After the founding of the University of Chicago, the relationship between Rockefeller and Harper began to deteriorate, for Harper was spending too much money trying to expand the school too quickly. He wanted the school to be a major establishment, and he was doing all he could to achieve his dream. He was spending a lot of money, however, and Rockefeller had to keep providing funds for the university. He was initially reluctant to give more money, but he would eventually give in and hand out the funds.

When Harper once said that no well-run school could be run free of a deficit, Rockefeller and Gates were outraged. Although Rockefeller suffered a lot of stress and had health problems at this time, he still said that it was the "best investment I ever made."

He had to constantly keep spending money, which was very difficult for him to do. Rockefeller was a very thrifty person who did not take money lightly. He did not spend freely and was always very strict about how much he spent. When he was a young boy, he would keep track of the accounts for his family and had a ledger, the famous Ledger A, in which he jotted down all of his expenses no matter how small. He included his donations to the Baptist Church and all of the money he spent in that little book, something that he greatly cherished and kept in his safe. From the time Rockefeller was a young boy, saving and frugality had been pounded into his head by his mother and by the circumstances and necessities of his surroundings. Now, because of Harper, Rockefeller had to keep spending hundreds of thousands dollars.

The matter affected him greatly, and he became unhappy.

Rockefeller grew so ill that he would spend days in bed. He suffered from digestive problems and sometimes ate only crackers and drank milk, something that he actually liked. Rockefeller grew so stressed that he needed to relax, and he took a few months off to recuperate. He worked with other workers near his home, but he was able to relax, had fun, ate his crackers and milk, and his health was restored not very long afterward, but he was not very eager to return to work.

He considered retirement, but could not and continued work until 1897.

When he got back on his feet, he attended a gathering where William Harper spoke. During Harper's speech, he turned to Rockefeller and addressed him on a matter of paying for something the school needed. Rockefeller simply smiled but was actually extremely uncomfortable with that prospect.

During the gathering, Rockefeller stood up and gave a short talk to the other people who had attended. They cheered heartily, and he was seen as a hero.

He had been considered a villain, vilified for how he had established Standard Oil and for his business strategies, but now he was seen as an idol—a hero.

In the end, when Rockefeller had had enough of Harper's overspending and leaving the school with a deficit, he decided to do things without going through him. He had Thomas Wakefield Goodspeed, who was a secretary on the University of Chicago's board, and Henry Rusty hold a meeting with Frederick Gates and Rockefeller Jr. Rockefeller himself did not go to the meeting and let his representative take care of everything.

In the end, the relationship between Rockefeller and Harper was tarnished. Harper was not to talk about money, but one story indicates that since he could not mention money or even bring up the topic of getting more money from Rockefeller, he would resort to asking for money during prayer in front of him.

Chapter 14 The Final Chapter in Greatness

"If your only goal is to become rich, you will never achieve it."

— John D. Rockefeller

During the late nineteenth century when Rockefeller was in his fifties, he suffered from a disease that would cause the loss of all or just some hair from one's body. Rockefeller lost all of his and started wearing toupees. He would change this toupee regularly to ones with longer hair to make it look as if his hair were growing. It wasn't just the hair on his face. It was everywhere. He had lost his hair around the time Standard Oil was getting bombarded in the press and in the courts.

After Rockefeller's wife passed away in 1915 from a heart attack, Rockefeller spent the next twenty-two years of his life having fun. He played golf, gave dimes to people, and went for a drive in the countryside every afternoon. He and another person would go, each in one car. Rockefeller always sat in the back of one of the cars with two women, one on each side. In his old days, Rockefeller was a much more relaxed old man who took slight pleasure in the company of younger women. He would invite them to play golf with him and go on drives.

In his later years, Rockefeller was as childish as a boy of nine. He hadn't been able to enjoy childhood when he was young, living as he did under the roof of a messed-up father and in a household always suffering from uncertainty and discomfort. In his eighties and nineties, he enjoyed life and relaxed. He eventually transferred the Rockefeller fortune to his son John D. Rockefeller Jr.

His long and fulfilling life came to an end on May 23, 1937, in the Casements on Ormond Beach in Florida. He was just short of ninety-eight years old.

At the time of his passing, Rockefeller's wealth equaled 2 percent of the American economy.

Today, he would have been worth between $250 and $300 billion.

Ida Tarbell, the reporter and author who hounded Rockefeller, had written much about him. None of it was complementary or kind, and she was certain that the motivation behind his success was attributable to his greed for money. It was a simplistic assumption that was incorrect.

What motivated Rockefeller was not money or the luxury it afforded. Money was just a consequence, and real wealth was not measured in how much one could buy or earn. Rather, it was measured by how much one did. Money was just a metric of that. The distinction is rare among the billionaire wannabes of today, but it is nonetheless a window into one of the world's most unique minds.

One should note that Rockefeller was pragmatic about his approach to work, success, and wealth. He was not driven by the reward but by the success of the endeavor. The reward was merely an afterthought. This is a difficult concept to comprehend in a world of stock traders and fast-money con artists who are looking to make a quick buck and then take it easy for the rest of their lives. Such men as Rockefeller, Carnegie, Morgan, and others worldwide were and are not done once they make their money. They reinvent themselves and go on to the next success. If they start something and fail, they get back up and keep going.

You have to ask yourself and contemplate the answer to the simple question of what does it take for someone such as Rockefeller to start from nothing and end up with everything. You have to evaluate your answer and ask yourself whether you want to emulate his own steps or in your particular limited way in your own life.

Conclusion

The story of John D. Rockefeller's life is deep and detailed that shows how a man whose background was most uncomfortable and terrible came to be one of the most successful and accomplished in the world and the world's richest man.

Rockefeller created the Standard Oil empire through hard work, determination, and perseverance. He may not have been completely honest in creating Standard Oil and the way he ran his business, but he did what he had to to make it the most successful oil company in the world.

Rockefeller's life was full of happiness, sadness, stress, and sickness. He despised his father, a rogue con man and bigamist who ruined his mother's life. He was very close to his mother and to his wife and was very serious about his morals. He never drank a single drop of alcohol, and he was an extremely pious and devout Baptist.

By the time he passed, he was just under ninety-eight years old and a happy, accomplished man.

John Davison Rockefeller had worked hard for every single penny he earned and for every single article of luxury he received and deserved. He made his fortune not for money's sake but to help the world and be a success. He changed the way America worked and had a significant role in its development and maybe even in how the world developed. When Rockefeller died, he had left his mark on it.

Indirectly, he caused the founding of one of the largest oil companies in the world: Royal Dutch Shell. It was established because the owners of the companies that merged to form the Shell Oil Company were uniting to be stronger against Standard Oil. So, you could say that it was because of him that the Shell Oil Company came into existence.

The lesson we can learn from Rockefeller's life is that being successful and being rich is never about the wealth or the money but the success and the accomplishment.

If someone is tempted to take his achievements lightly, forgetting his stressful childhood, his disappointments, and his relentless pursuit of objectives amidst seemingly insurmountable challenges, think about the world without him and think about how far we would have come without his contribution to the development of the oil and gas industry. It is not about the hundreds of millions of dollars that he amassed in his lifetime. That is not necessarily what makes him great. Rather, it is the uphill battles he fought and in the process changed the world we came from into the world we now live in

Unlike those who die rich but in actual fact are poor because the money they had was either dishonestly accumulated or inherited, John D. Rockefeller passed away wealthier than his monetary wealth because money earned through hard work and effort means more than money.

As Rockefeller said, "If you're only goal is to become rich, you will never achieve it."

If you enjoyed learning about John D Rockefeller I would be forever grateful if you could leave a review. Reviews are the best way to help give feedback to newer authors and also help your fellow readers find the books worth reading. Thanks in advance!

Made in the USA
Thornton, CO
08/25/23 15:24:05

8297f9c5-39f6-4840-ad1f-e6b3de4b70f3R01